THE
IRISH COUNTRYWOMEN'S ASSOCIATION
Book of Home and Family

ABOUT THE ICA

Founded in May 1910, the aim of the ICA was 'to improve the standard of life in rural Ireland through education and co-operative effort'. Today the ICA has 700 local Guilds in cities, towns and rural areas throughout Ireland. They continue to offer support and fun as well as opportunities to make friends, learn new skills and contribute to the wider community. Every day, the women share with each other nuggets of advice, tried-and-tested methods and practical help, and they hope this book will pass on some of that knowledge to you.

The Irish Countrywomen's Association

BOOK OF HOME AND FAMILY

Practical Know-How and Pearls of Wisdom from Irish Women

General Editor Aoife Carrigy

GILL & MACMILLAN

GILL & MACMILLAN

Hume Avenue, Park West, Dublin 12

with associated companies throughout the world

www.gillmacmillanbooks.ie

© IRISH COUNTRYWOMEN'S TRUST 2013

978 07171 5771 6

General Editor Aoife Carrigy

Index compiled by Eileen O'Neill

Design and print origination by Tanya M Ross, www.elementinc.ie

Illustrations by Tanya M Ross, www.elementinc.ie

Printed by Printer Trento Srl, Italy

Photography © Joanne Murphy, www.joanne-murphy.com

Styled by Carly Horan and Blondie Horan, www.styledwithlove.ie

Photographer's assistant Líosa MacNamara

PROPS SUPPLIED BY

Ashley Cottage Interiors, Tralee, Co Kerry

Historic Interiors, Oberstown, Lusk, Co Dublin. T: +353 (1) 843 7174; E: killian@historicinteriors.net

Moss Cottage, Main Street, Dundrum, Dublin 14. T: +353 (1) 215 7696; E: hello@mosscottage.ie; W: www.mosscottage.ie

1 3 5 4 2

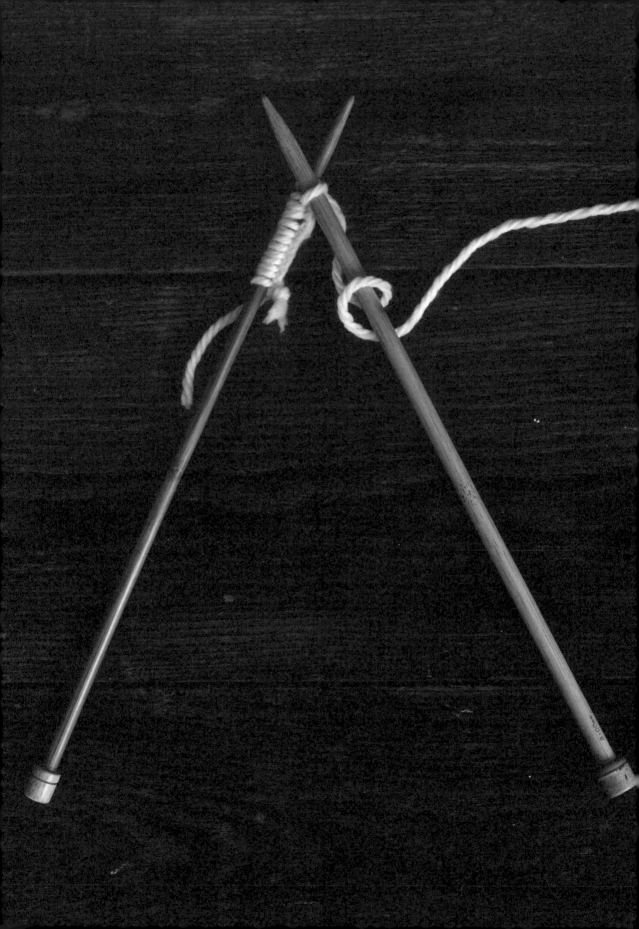

Contents

Introduction

In 2012, we published *The ICA Cookbook*, a collection of treasured recipes gathered from ICA members across the country. We wanted to pass on these much-loved dishes to a new generation of home-cooks, to capture in a book the smells and flavours of real Irish kitchens so that they might be recreated in homes far and wide.

As National President of the Irish Countrywomen's Association, I was very pleased to have been asked to write the foreword for *The ICA Cookbook*, and even more pleased that the book was so well received at home and abroad. The enthusiastic response got us to thinking how much more collective practical advice the ICA women have to offer the next generation. Young parents running households today are often shocked to learn that the role is akin to that of CEO of a small company. There's the budgeting, stock management, planning and organisation to keep on top of. There are the manual and practical demands such as keeping the house well, cooking, cleaning and maintaining your appliances. And then there's that little bit of magic needed to make the home a happy one – the special touches and clever tricks that seemed to come naturally to all of our mammies.

These days, many young folk no longer live next door to their mother to whom they might call around for advice on everything from how to get a stain out of a dress to the trials and tribulations of married life. My own daughters are often asked for household and budgeting tips from college friends who know their mother is in the ICA. Yet all that advice is there for the asking, in homes all around the country. We decided to put out a call to our 11,000-strong ICA members to share their tips, skills, cherished 'how tos' and nuggets of wisdom on how to run a happy, harmonious home. And so *The ICA Book of Home and Family* was born.

As we sifted through submissions from hundreds of women representing ICA Guilds right across the country, I have personally been inspired in surprising ways (I'm currently planning to invest in a few hens for my own garden) and have learnt many things I never knew. My mother died before I had the chance or indeed the interest to garner her tips and advice about running a home and family. I thought I was always going to have time to learn from her, and then, when I needed to know – when I was setting out to make my own home for my own family – there was no-one there to tell me.

Had she lived longer, I might have a few more additions to add to the book myself (although I'm pleased to see my failsafe method for dealing with smelly shoes appear on page 160!). As it is, I am delighted to be able to rely on the resourceful members of the ICA for nuggets of wisdom and helpful hints on everything from how to clean leather to how to keep your hair shiny. I love that most of the tips in this book are easy to master and cheap to reproduce, often using everyday household items like lemon juice and vinegar in place of an array of expensive cleaning products. Many of these tips have been passed down by mothers and grandmothers from a time when frugality and resourcefulness were key survival tools, as they are becoming again today for so many.

I have also enjoyed reading personal memories from back in the day. One member writes about growing up as one of 10 children on the hills near Ballyroan in Co Laois and how her mother knew everything from how to sew and knit all their clothes to how to make up remedies for ailing family members. Another in Kildare recollects her parents bartering with neighbours for milk and potatoes, eggs and vegetables so that they never went hungry despite rarely buying any food.

Life has changed greatly since those days but we can learn so much from them. We are busier today than ever – many of us have full- or part-time jobs outside the home – and yet we still want to keep our home in great shape so that it is somewhere we look forward to returning to at the end of our long day.

Running a home remains a serious job demanding specialised knowledge which we are not all born knowing, and which we are often only ready to learn once we have left our original family home. Making a house a home can be a source of great pleasure, both in the creation and the enjoyment of its harmony. Doing it well is both an art and a skill. We hope you will enjoy dipping in and out of this book and calling on the help of all the home-makers who went before you. We have much to learn from them in so many ways. Let's use and thereby preserve their know-how for the next generation to treasure.

Liz Wall
National President of the Irish Countrywomen's Association

We are bombarded today with ideals of the perfect home-maker. Rather than adding to those demands, *The ICA Cookbook* and now this follow-up home-maker's manual provide a reliable reference source for when you need trusted advice rooted in real life experience. The truth is that there is no one perfect way to make a Christmas cake, nor to poach an egg, nor to keep a home shipshape. To the contrary, there are many alternative ways and the secret is in finding the particular tricks that work for you and your household.

A quick glance at the list of contributors will tell you that this is very much a crowd-sourced book. Literally hundreds of ICA women added their tuppence worth to the discussion of how the important job of making a house a home might become that little bit easier and more satisfying. Many of these women have strikingly different approaches to the one task. Take the challenge of how to deal with garden slugs. Some deter the creatures with copper wiring or woo them to a happy end with beer baths. Others get straight to business with a torch and a pair of scissors, and let the birds dispatch the gruesome remains. As a reader, you can choose which of these tried and tested tips would work best for you.

Just as this book is made up of the real life experience of many different home-makers from all over the country, so too will it be referenced by all sorts of different home-makers, many of whom may not consider home-making to be their primary role but for whom the home is still a precious refuge worth nurturing. Our society, our lifestyles and our individual roles within them have changed dramatically in recent generations, but each one of us still deserves a home we can feel comfortable in and look forward to coming home to. Whether that home is in a rented apartment or a mortgaged semi-d, whether we live alone, share with other adults or head up a family household, there's something for all of us to learn from the collective experience of the mammies of Ireland and their mammies before them.

These no-nonsense women are not here to set up impossible ideals for us to feel guilty about not achieving. There's a good reason that the two birthday cakes featured here involve zero baking and can each be constructed in about five minutes flat. These women's practical experience tells us that yes, keeping hens is a worthwhile endeavour but it can take its toll on your garden; that relationships do take effort, and so too does keeping on top of laundry and cleaning and shopping and cooking and gardening. But they are here to reassure us that there are handy little tricks to staying on top of it all, and that the rewards make it worth all that effort.

The short-and-sweet ICA motto is 'Deeds not Words', and so it is little surprise that, when we put the call out to all ICA members to send us their contributions for this book, the bulk of that response was practical advice for the chapters on catering for family occasions and managing the house. After all, the kitchen is the heart of the home and keeping a well-run house is all about making space within those walls for love and life to blossom. Perhaps many Irish mammies are more comfortable expressing their love through deeds than words? Could it be that knowing how to make the perfect cuppa is in fact knowing how to tell someone you care, or that they're very welcome in your home, or that you'll always have an ear for their worries?

The bulk of this book may be made up of practical 'how-tos', but they are infused with that most important ingredient for making a house a home: love. How to nurture the love in a marriage and find time to enjoy the love of a young family. How to learn to love yourself and how you look, and to value the love of your extended family and friends. How to express that love through home-made gifts or hospitality or a nurturing tonic – or indeed, a perfect cuppa. Suggestions for all of these important 'how-tos' are peppered throughout this book also, and frame the more prosaic chapters at the heart of it.

Whatever it is that makes you reach for this book – a moment's lull in a busy day when you're seeking a little insight to muse over, or a particular challenge that needs practical guidance – you can do so knowing that these women know their stuff. If *The ICA Cookbook* was "akin to having not just your own mammy on speed dial but rather a whole host of mammies and grannies from all over the country, each sharing their own words of wisdom and precious firsthand experiences", then this crowd-sourced ICA *Book of Home and Family* is like having access to the ICA chat room where no question is too small to ask and there's an easy answer for every problem.

With Love

Chapter 1
Love, Marriage & Family

MAKING A HOUSE A HOME · LOVE & MARRIAGE
CHILDREN & EXTENDED FAMILIES

Making a House a Home

Your house is your home. Make it that and don't stress if it's not like your high-powered neighbour's home: it's your happy home, and the heart of your family life. It will be a nicer place to be if it is full of laughter and fun than if it is spotless but soul-less.

We all want our homes to look their best, and this book is full of first-hand tips and advice on how to achieve the smooth running of your household. But rather than trying to do everything yourself and grumbling about it, instead it is better for everyone if you gently enlist the help of all family members. After all, the home is the heart of the family, but it is the family that makes the home.

Finishing Touches

It was always the little magic touches that our mothers sprinkled around every room that really helped to make a house a home. You can bring your own magic to your home by paying attention to some of the sights and scents and finishing touches that give each room its special ambiance.

A room that has been unused or closed up for a while can become musty. A tray of cat litter will help prevent musty odours building up. Or to create your own DIY air freshener, combine one teaspoon of bicarbonate of soda, two tablespoons of vinegar and two cups of clean water in a spray bottle. Once the mixture has stopped foaming, replace the spray top, shake well and use as a spray air freshener as needed. You could add a couple of drops of essential oil to scent the cleaner. To clear the smell of smoky rooms, dip a tea towel in vodka and shake vigorously around the room. A little bicarbonate of soda in ashtrays also helps to reduce odours by extinguishing cigarettes quickly and avoiding having them smoulder on.

Burning candles helps to keep the air fresh as well as adding ambiance. You can stretch the lifespan of candles by chilling them in the freezer for a few hours before using. To clean a wax-covered candlestick without damaging the surface beneath the wax, pop it in the freezer for an hour or two after which the wax will chip off very easily. To refill, dip the base of each candle into very hot water to soften before securing into the candlestick.

And while you might think life is too short to be polishing light bulbs, not only will they give a better light for the room (especially if cleaned with white spirits) but you can also rub in a little of your favourite perfume or essential oil to give off a pleasant smell when you switch it on.

> **"** *My mam never forgot the advice she got from my dad's mother when they were first married: make yourself comfortable in your own home.* **"**
> Margaret Murphy,
> Waterford

Recipe for a Happy Home
"Take
2 spoons of love
1 cup of loyalty
3 spoons of hope
2 cups of forgiveness
2 spoons of friendship
1 cup of forever and
4 heaped spoons of laughter.
Mix all together
and the end result will be
a happy home."
Kathleen Gorman, Laois

❝ *Níl aon tinteán mar
do thinteán féin
(there's no hearth like
your own hearth).* ❞
Lismullen Guild Members,
Meath

Back in the Day...

"The principal use of Granny's apron was to protect the dress underneath. But along with that, it also served as a holder for removing hot pans from the oven. It was great for drying children's tears and on occasion was even used for cleaning dirty ears. From the chicken house, the apron carried eggs, fussy chicks and sometimes half-hatched eggs to be finished in the warming oven. When company came, the apron was a handy hiding place for shy children.

When the weather was cold, Granny wrapped it around her arms. Those big aprons wiped many a perspiring brow, bent over a hot stove. Sticks and kindling wood were brought into the kitchen in that apron, and from the garden it carried all sorts of vegetables. After the peas were shelled, it carried out the hulls, and in autumn it was used to bring in apples that had fallen from trees.

When unexpected company drove up the road, it was surprising how much furniture that old apron could dust in a matter of seconds. When dinner was ready, Granny walked out onto the porch, waved her apron and the men knew it was time to come in from the fields.

It will be a long time before someone invents something that will replace that old-time apron which served so many purposes."
Winnie McCarron, Monaghan

Love & Marriage

There's an old saying that you shouldn't marry the one that you can live with, but rather you should marry the one that you can't live without. Either way, marriage can be something of a marathon after the hop and skip of the romantic love affair that often precedes it.

Marriages take work, but much of that work can be great fun. It is important always to celebrate each other's birthdays, anniversaries and other significant events together, even if you are short on money or time. The truth is that very little money is needed and simple things work best. As well as the special occasions, set aside some quality time once a week to spend with your partner (without the children if you have any). Take turns to plan it: a late dinner, a film in front of the fire, or some music, a glass of wine and a conversation – it doesn't matter what you do together, as long as it is something you enjoy doing together. The most important thing to sustain after having children is that precious time spent together. It doesn't have to be the same night each week but never skip a week. The regular connection will be needed to help you both through difficult times.

Many unnecessary arguments can be avoided by counting to ten before retorting when you're angry. It can be hard to do but can help to avoid a much bigger row. Never let the sun go down on your anger, but always try to make up any quarrel before bedtime. Remember that gratitude and forgiveness are key to a good life, and that forgiveness benefits not just the one forgiven but the one who forgives. A little humility can go a long way too: the quickest way to forget others' faults and shortcomings is by taking the time to remember some of your own.

66 *Love is blind and marriage is an eye opener.* 99
Mary Butler, Kilkenny

Maintain a Good Relationship

Remember...

❧ ... to approach love and cooking with reckless abandon

❧ ... to take into account that great love and great achievements involve great risk

❧ ... that a loving atmosphere in your home is the foundation for your life

❧ ... that it takes seventy-two muscles to frown and only twenty-three to smile, and smiling has much more pleasurable results

❧ ... to help without being asked

❧ ... that asking for help doesn't mean you are weak, but rather intelligent

❧ ... to buy gifts that say I love you, not pots and pans or DIY tools

❧ ... to fight fair, resist interrupting and take turns talking

❧ ... to deal only with the current situation in disagreements and to resist bringing up the past

❧ ... that honesty is important but so is tact

❧ ... to focus on what is right and not who is right

❧ ... to cool down before you speak when you are angry

❧ ... to admit when you are wrong and shut up when you are right

❧ ... that a good relationship needs 50/50 participation, with each of you giving 100 per cent

❧ ... that your interpretation of what you see and hear is just that – your interpretation

❧ ... to criticise the performance, not the performer

❧ ... that worry comes from the belief that you are powerless

❧ ... that hoping and wishing are poor excuses for not doing

❧ ... to spend some time alone every day

❧ ... to open your arms to change, but without letting go of your values

❧ ... that silence is sometimes the best answer

❧ ... that the best relationship is one in which your love for each other exceeds your need for each other

❧ ... to strive for an honourable life, so that when you get older and think back upon it you'll be in a position to enjoy it a second time

❧ ... to follow the three Rs: respect for self, respect for others and responsibility for all your actions

❧ ... that every survival kit should include a sense of humour

Children &
Extended Families

Young children are great fun and a pleasure to be with. Enjoy them. They grow up so fast and you never get this time back: it is clichéd because it is true. Make the most of what precious family time you can squeeze in and remember there is lots of free stuff to be enjoyed out there. Seek it out. It is those fun times together that they will remember, not the fancy toys and clothes that you might struggle to buy.

Try to sit down most nights for a family dinner. As well as encouraging healthy eating habits, it is such an important time for a family to share, a chance to talk together about everyone's day. Ask each person to list out five or six things they are happy about that day. It could be as small as 'I'm happy that there is cake for dessert' or as significant as 'I'm happy I won a prize at school' or 'I'm happy that Granny is out of hospital'. It encourages the family to concentrate on the positives and to share them with each other. Often something important to one family member may have been overlooked by the rest of the family.

Including the extended family in regular family events is a great way of banking memories. Your own parents won't be around forever and you will miss them when they are gone. Invite them over to watch a favourite film together on a rainy afternoon, with popcorn and all; dust out the old Scrabble set and get the competitive spirits going; or go for gentle walks to tire out young children and let their grandparents read them a favourite book before going to sleep.

Dinner on the Hob

Coordinating family schedules can be tricky, but there's nothing like coming home to a warm home-cooked dinner. Reheating in a microwave tends to dry out food. If one of the family is delayed for dinner, put their plate over a large pan of boiling water, reduce to a low simmer and cover the plate with another plate. The dinner will be kept warm and perfectly moist. Be sure to keep topping up with water so that the pot doesn't run dry. A couple of coins or pebbles in the base of the pot will rattle about when the water is running low, alerting you to top up before the last of the water is boiled off.

Mind the Pennies...

Cover new schoolbooks (not the workbooks but any textbooks which don't require being written into) with leftover wallpaper or heavy-duty brown paper so that they can be re-used next year.

Dealing with Challenges

While your family can be the source of so much pleasure, life doesn't always go exactly as we have anticipated. When young babies arrive, there can be a few surprises in store. Breastfeeding doesn't always just happen and can take lots of effort and persistence. It is beneficial in so many ways and the bonding time is priceless. Don't give up without getting help and support, but if it's not happening for you, don't beat yourself up either.

Recognise that there will be many more challenges along the way, and sometimes it can all become too much to juggle. Ask for help from your friends, parents, in-laws and neighbours when you are struggling. They will be happy to be of help – even if it's just an hour or two's relief, or someone else to do the school run every once in a while – and you can always return the favours later, when life is feeling more manageable. Remind yourself that every situation changes and evolves, and that in a few years' time you will be in a different place.

If you are staying at home with the children and your partner is working, it is important to remember that *both* of you will most likely have been working hard all day. Try to arrange it so that each of you has some downtime. Perhaps you could let your partner sit down and relax with a cup of tea when they come home from work. And then you could enjoy a quiet moment while your partner does bath time? It's about sharing the responsibilities, not offloading them, and you'll be better able to enjoy it all if you work as a team and support each other.

As your family grows older, you will learn that you must never underestimate a child's ability to get up to more mischief. Don't expect your child to be perfect, because none of us are. It's worth remembering too that more learning occurs outside of school than inside, and that while you want them to get the most potential out of life, there are many ways to skin a cat, and many ways to live a life. Encourage your children's strengths, and allow them their weaknesses and mistakes – we all make them. You, as a parent, will make many too, as we all did. The tragedy is in not learning from them.

Managing Budgets

Money troubles sometimes come from unforeseen circumstances, but more often they are due to bad managing of whatever resources you do have. Our grandmothers would have always kept three tins of money: one for electricity, one for rent and one for fuel. When they received the household money every week, they would first set aside enough in those tins to cover the bills and would then live on what was left. For modern families, the same can apply. Set aside enough money every month to pay your essential bills, and then you know what you have left to work with.

Consider keeping a money jar beside main light switches and fining family members each time a light is left on in an empty room. Be careful not to be wooed by 'bargains': a thing is dear at any price if you do not need it. Try to live by the old adage, 'Neither a Borrower Nor a Lender Be', and stay within your current means as much as is possible.

Chapter 2

The Home-maker's Diary

Weekly & Monthly Home-maker's Planner

The most important trick up the clever home-maker's sleeve is the ability to be proactive rather than reactive. Running around worrying about all the little jobs you haven't yet got to doing is no fun. On the other hand, there's a surprising satisfaction in ticking things off a list in good time, and knowing that you've allocated a time for dealing with all those little details that could otherwise slide indefinitely. With that in mind, and to help to keep you on top of things, we've supplied you with suggestions for tasks to be tackled throughout the year.

We've suggested how to start your own planner and dropped in some ideas for things to do each month. However, only you will know when makes the most sense for you to tackle all your tasks and so we recommend that you create your own home-maker's planner and add in what makes sense for you. It's handy to have a weekly cleaning roster to refer to, and to share out the tasks among different household members. For the larger monthly tasks you might like to spread them out evenly, or you might prefer to set aside one week a month during which you can undertake these less regular tasks. It's about figuring out what works best for you and your household.

WEEKLY TO-DO LIST

Set aside some daily 'me-time' to do something for yourself (p150).

Set aside some weekly quality time to spend with your partner (p5).

Share at least one weekly meal with the family (p8).

Attempt to dispatch the week's laundry (p32).

Change bed linen and hoover bedroom floors (p45).

Change or wash dishcloths (p51).

Clean bathroom: sinks, baths, toilet, floor, mirrors (p42).

Clean kitchen sink and drains (p51).

Dust surfaces (p20).

Hoover carpets and wash floors (p27).

MONTHLY TO-DO LIST

Set aside some monthly quality time to spend with your friends (p150).

Clean fridge (p47) and breadbin (p46).

Clean oven (p50).

Clean rubbish bins (p47).

Clean washing machine (p33).

Polish wooden and leather furniture (p24 & 26).

Refresh carpets (p27) and soft furnishings (p28).

Refresh microwave (p50).

Run dishwasher on empty for maintenance (p52).

Tackle bathroom mildew (p43).

Wash windows (p44).

Annual Home-maker's Planner

BI-MONTHLY TO-DO LIST (every two months)

Clean steam iron (p40).

Clean tumble dryer (p37).

Defrost ice-box and deep-clean fridge (p48).

Run washing machine on empty for maintenance (p33).

QUARTERLY TO-DO LIST (every three months)

Air and/or wash curtains (p28).

Clean hearth tiles and marble fireplaces (p26).

Deep-clean bathroom: showerheads (p43), grouting (p43), shower curtains (p44) and drains (p44).

Deep-clean kitchens: clean tiles (p22), clean out cupboards, replace soda in fridge (p47).

Defrost freezer (p48).

Deweed driveways (p130).

Polish ornaments and cutlery (p24).

Turn mattresses (p45) and air bedrooms (p45).

Wash carpets and deep-clean floors (p27).

Wash foam pillows (p45).

Wash soft-furnishing covers (p28).

BI-ANNUAL TO-DO LIST (every six months)

Clean and service lawnmower before and after winter storage (p130).

Declutter kitchen cupboards (p53).

Recycle or store away seasonal wardrobes (p159).

ANNUAL TO-DO LIST (every year)

Clean and touch up skirting boards and paintwork (p64).

Have chimney cleaned professionally (p26).

Store away garden tools properly for winter (p130).

Wash walls and ceilings (p29).

Jan	Celebrate Nollaig na mBan			
Feb		Celebrate St Valentine's Day		
March			Celebrate St Patrick's Day	
April				Clean up garden after winter
May	Store away winter woollens	Plant out summer bedding		
June			Celebrate St John's Eve	
July				Pack a picnic
Aug		Buy and cover school books		
Sept	Store away summer clothes		Harvest home-grown fruit and vegetables	
Oct		Store away garden tools		Celebrate Halloween
Nov			Make Christmas cake and pudding	
Dec	Watch the Late Late Toy Show			Celebrate Christmas

Chapter 3

Household Management

CLEANING · LAUNDRY · BATHROOM · BEDROOM
KITCHEN · MAINTENANCE & DIY

Cleaning

There are those who claim that life's too short to be spent sweeping and scrubbing and dusting and buffing – and they have a point, of course. Like life itself, a home is there to be lived in and enjoyed. But how much more enjoyable is life when played out in a clean, orderly environment, with 'a place for everything and everything in its place'?

While there is good sense in the idea of a spring clean, or of allocating certain household jobs to certain times of year, it's worth remembering that all long journeys are made up of small steps. If you allow everything to build up with a view to giving the whole house a thorough cleaning every three months, you and your family will come to dread those periods of upheaval when the house is turned inside-out and made uncomfortable for all. A better approach is to keep the house clean by daily attention to the small things, and not to allow it to get into a state of dirt and disorder. Not only will the work seem less daunting, but you'll enjoy the special satisfaction of a well-ordered house year-round rather than only at certain times of the year. What's more, your children will learn the habits of order and neatness. It is far easier to repeat good habits learnt young than to change bad ones later in life. Write up a list of weekly cleaning duties, and be sure to delegate fairly but firmly. And if you can afford it, consider hiring a cleaner, even occasionally, to help with the deeper cleaning.

Of course, it's all about balance – so try to remember your priorities too. The aim should be for a comfortable house which gives yourself and your family pleasure, not a perfect house which gets in the way of you having fun.

Cut Down on Chemicals

Some people are particularly sensitive to chemical products but even if you don't suffer from asthma and allergies, it is a good idea to reduce exposure by using as many natural cleaning products as possible – and it will help the environment and your budget to boot. There are some great products on the market or you can make up some simple solutions yourself with kitchen staples such as vinegar, salt, lemon and bicarbonate of soda. You'll find lots of ideas throughout this book.

To make up your own all-purpose cleaner for use on any hard surface, mix 500ml (1 pint) of water with two tablespoons of lemon juice, a tablespoon of bicarbonate of soda, a tablespoon of borax and half a teaspoon of washing-up liquid in a spray bottle.

However, if you have to use products that may aggravate allergies, make sure the room you are cleaning is well-ventilated and never mix cleaning products with each other: some chemicals may react adversely if mixed, creating toxic fumes. If one product fails to do the job, wash the surface or item to which you applied it before using another. Always store your cleaning products in a safe place, keep the products in their original containers and follow the manufacturer's directions.

Dusting & Polishing

Remember that there's a sensible order in which to do your housework. Surfaces should be dusted first, then washed and finally polished. It's best to sweep before dusting when cleaning hard floors, as the broom will raise the dust – and you certainly don't want to make extra work for yourself.

Thankfully there are many handy tricks for making less work for yourself. Adding a little fabric conditioner to a duster before polishing will help keep dust at bay, as will the combination of a teaspoon each of vinegar and glycerine mixed into a litre (1¾ pints) of water. Just dab it onto a soft cloth and wipe it over your furniture.

Remember too that there's dusters and there's dusters! You could buy a purpose-made duster that is treated to attract dust or you could do as women have for many years and make your own from old scraps of clothes or even old socks (just slip onto your hand and away you go). Whatever you use, it will work best if you treat it in advance. Soak it in one part lemon oil to eight parts water, or in an eggcupful of equal parts paraffin and vinegar. Then just wring it out and leave to dry. Once treated, your duster will give furniture an extra gleam, absorb dust better and help to keep it from gathering on TV screens, computers and glass table tops.

It's worth having a few more weapons in your dusting arsenal. Keep a soft-bristled brush handy for dusting book cases, stereo systems, computers, ornaments and ornate silverware. A baby's hairbrush is particularly useful for the ridges and grooves of pleated lampshades: the long soft hairs get right into the crevices but won't harm delicate fabric. Hard-to-dust plant leaves can be cleaned more thoroughly by rubbing with the inside of a banana skin. Piano keys scrub up well with a damp cloth and a little toothpaste, wiped dry and buffed with a soft cloth.

While pets can be such a joy to have around, they don't always make life easy for us owners. Rid upholstery of pesky pet hair by wiping with a slightly dampened sponge or rubber gloves. Alternatively, wrap a little sellotape around your fingers sticky-side outward and rub over the hairs. (This works a treat for lint and hairs on clothes too.)

66 *A good start is half the work.* 99
Mary Butler, Kilkenny

Back in the Day...

"We always had geese at home for Christmas: one for Christmas Day and one for New Year's Day. We also had two ducks for the 12th day or 'Little Christmas'. My mother always kept the two wings of both birds and put them to dry with a weight on them. They made great dusters to remove cobwebs and were the best to clean out the cooker and to get into narrow places."
Betty Gorman, Laois

Handle Various Surfaces

Marble

To remove light stains simply rub with undiluted white wine vinegar, or mixed with one part salt. Either way, leave the vinegar on the surface for a few minutes before rinsing thoroughly with clean water, rubbing with a wedge of lemon and wiping dry. Lemon juice is also useful for lifting limescale, rust and other general stains.

Metal

Use a little vodka on a sponge to wipe stainless steel clean and keep it sparkling. Lemon juice can be used neat or diluted to clean tarnish or limescale from metal surfaces such as brass and copper. If you need more abrasive action, try a piece of lemon dipped in salt.

Porcelain

To clean porcelain surfaces and remove light stains, rub with cream of tartar sprinkled on a damp cloth. Works well on light stains. Bicarbonate of soda dissolved in warm water is also great for porcelain or enamel fixtures as well as for stainless steel, chrome, fibreglass and ceramics.

Tabletops

Wipe plastic surfaces with a cleaning duster dampened with a solution of half vinegar and half water. If a beeswax-polished surface becomes scratched or spotted, rub the scratches or spots with white vinegar and polish again with beeswax whilst the surface is still wet.

Tiles

If a hard water film has formed on tiles or glass, rub the surface with undiluted white vinegar, leave for fifteen minutes and rinse thoroughly. To remove the white patches that form on quarry tiles, mix a tablespoon of vinegar with a pint of water. Soak a cloth in the mix, wring gently and use to scrub the tiles. Allow to dry before deciding if you need to apply a second scrub.

Ornaments & Cutlery

Every once in a while (preferably not two hours before guests arrive, but rather during some downtime when the house is quiet and your favourite music is playing), take the time to lay out some old newspaper, collect together all your brass and silver and give them a bit of elbow juice to get them sparkling again.

You can make your own all-purpose home-made metal scrub that is suitable for brass, copper, chrome and pewter. Combine one tablespoon of flour with two teaspoons of salt and just enough vinegar to bind into a thick paste. Apply to the metal with a soft cloth to scrub clean, rinse and dry, and finally buff with a separate cleaning cloth to bring up the shine. You could add a little olive oil to prevent future tarnishing.

SILVER: A tube of white toothpaste, some warm water and an old soft-bristled toothbrush are all you need to get your silverware sparkling. The brush will tackle the nooks and crannies of most ornaments and for cleaning cutlery, toothpaste has the edge over the risk of silver polish residue ruining your guest's dinner. Simply rub on with a sponge and rinse off with warm soapy water. Alternatively, to clean a lot of silver cutlery in a hurry, line a washing-up bowl with strips of tin foil, place the silver cutlery on top and cover with boiling water. Stir in several tablespoons of bicarbonate of soda and leave to soak for 10 minutes. You could also try soaking in the water in which you cooked potatoes, which helps remove tarnish from silver.

BRASS: A salt and lemon juice scrub (three parts to one) will clean brass well, as will very sour milk, while olive oil brings a great shine. Or use wet ashes to clean brass door-knobs and candle sticks.

BRONZE: Never wash bronze ornaments, but simply dust with a muslin or silk duster and a soft brush for any fiddly bits. If you need a deeper clean, sponge with stale beer, leave to dry and then polish with a chamois leather.

COPPER: Moisten a paper towel with a solution of equal parts lemon juice and vinegar and use to clean copper before polishing with a soft, dry duster.

OTHER BITS & BOBS: Rub gilt frames with white spirits to make them sparkle. Brighten zinc articles by washing in warm soapy water before buffing with a cloth soaked in white spirits.

Furniture & Fireplaces

As well as keeping surfaces dust-free and clean on a weekly basis, allocate the time to give various features such as fireplaces and furniture some regular TLC. It's easy not to notice the accumulation of dirt in your favourite wicker chair into which you love to flop, but you'll notice when it's looking as good as new again. A solution of warm water and washing soda is just the thing for cleaning wicker and cane furniture. Lemon juice and salt will also clean cane, while water applied with a plant spray will keep wicker supple.

WOODEN FURNITURE: There's something very beautiful about a well-loved piece of wooden furniture. A good all-purpose solution to help you both clean and polish wood is a mixture of two parts olive oil, three parts white spirits and four parts vinegar. Shake together thoroughly, apply with a cloth and finish off with a dry clean cloth. Linseed oil is a great friend to natural wood, helping to protect as well as rejuvenate and polish. To remove marks from and give renewed shine to stained wood, mix a teaspoon of salt into 300ml (½ pint) boiled linseed oil. Apply a few drops of this to a cotton cloth, rub over the marks and buff with a clean cloth.

Mahogany furniture is always best cleaned by continued rubbing. If you'd like to go so far as giving your furniture that 'French polish' beloved of cabinet makers, mix up a 850ml (1½ pint) of un-boiled linseed oil, 570ml (1 pint) of white spirits and a teaspoon of leaf sugar. Shake together thoroughly, apply with a flannel cloth and finish off with a dry, clean linen cloth. For oak furniture, washing in a little warm beer improves the colour and is far superior to soap and water. Once dry, polish with furniture cream or with your old friend, linseed oil. Dark wood can be cleaned with strong black coffee to help improve the colour, while varnish blackened with soot can be applied to make new furniture look older. For old furniture on which there is a build-up of wax and dirt, clean with one part vinegar to eight parts water and re-polish once dry.

If your precious wooden furniture has small scratches, don't despair. Try rubbing them with a shelled walnut, hazelnut or Brazil nut to see the scratches magically disappear. Shoe polish or soft crayons are also handy for disguising scratches on furniture; simply apply along the grain with a soft cloth. Meanwhile, deeper gouges can be disguised by brushing iodine into them.

Dealing with Marks & Stains

Treat water marks and ring marks on wood by rubbing with tooth paste. For stubborn ones, you can add some baking soda and then polish with a soft cloth. Waxed wood should be treated with white spirits, rubbing along the grain. Another technique is to spread mayonnaise over the mark and leave it to soak overnight before wiping off with a soft cloth. If you can't shift the marks, you could always disguise them by rubbing with cigarette ash or coloured shoe polish; use a cotton bud to apply.

Cigarette burns and ink stains can be gently rubbed away with some fine steel wool, followed by linseed oil to restore the colour. Or you could try removing these by rubbing with a little oxalic acid, but take care not to spread the acid over the wood more than is necessary and be sure to rinse well with warm water before polishing.

For those white marks made by heat or alcohol, rubbing around the mark with two drops of methylated spirit on a pad of cotton wool will move the surrounding polish over the mark and help to cover it. You could also try rubbing cigarette ash and vinegar on heat marks, or camphor spirit (if you can get your hands on any) which should be applied with a soft rag before polishing.

LEATHER FURNITURE

Leather furniture can look great – when it's looking great, that is. To keep it at its best, mix the white of an egg into a cup of milk and top up with cold water to make up a pint in total. Stir well and apply with a sponge, allow to dry and buff with a soft brush to make the leather shine like new. Olive oil is also great for moisturising and conditioning leather furniture and as a furniture polish in general, as is a combination of two parts linseed oil and one part vinegar. Apply evenly with a soft cloth and buff up with a silk rag.

Sometimes, however, your leather furniture will need more than a shine. White leather in particular needs regular cleaning. Dampen a cloth or sponge with toilet soap and rub in light circles to lift the dirt evenly. Be sure to wash off thoroughly with a clean damp cloth, and once dry, polish as above. (See p35 for more tips.)

FIREPLACES

Who doesn't warm to a blazing fire? One of the upsides of living in a moderate climate such as ours is that you get a chance to light it most months of the year. An open fire takes a bit of work, but there are ways you can cut down on it.

In an open solid-fuel fireplace, a rectangular biscuit tin placed under the fire grate into which most of the ashes can fall will make cleaning much easier and quicker. Just be sure that the ashes are completely cold before transferring to a plastic bag for disposal: the ash of peat briquettes in particular can contain smouldering remains for a surprisingly long time. If in doubt,

transfer to another cake tin to cool fully.

A clean chimney is something that gives you peace of mind rather than any aesthetic satisfaction, and while it's also important to have it cleaned professionally at least once a year, there are good practice tips worth building into your habits. Save your potato peelings, mix with a little salt and add to the grate once a week to cut down on sooty deposits in the chimney.

Hearth tiles will dull with time. To refresh, wash with a cloth moistened with vinegar and rinse off immediately, or dissolve a teaspoon of sugar in the juice of a lemon and apply to keep them bright. Burn marks on a marble fireplace can be lifted by rubbing with a cloth dampened with lemon juice and dipped in salt.

If your fireplace has glass doors, the inside panes can be cleaned easily with some vinegar-dampened newspaper. Simply wipe down for an instant non-streak clean.

Mind the Pennies...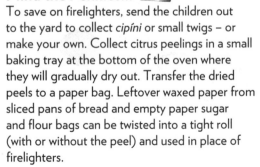

To save on firelighters, send the children out to the yard to collect *cipíní* or small twigs – or make your own. Collect citrus peelings in a small baking tray at the bottom of the oven where they will gradually dry out. Transfer the dried peels to a paper bag. Leftover waxed paper from sliced pans of bread and empty paper sugar and flour bags can be twisted into a tight roll (with or without the peel) and used in place of firelighters.

Floors & Carpets

A good carpet deserves a bit of love. A quick way to refresh your carpet is to sprinkle it liberally with bicarbonate of soda, leave for 20 minutes and hoover up the remains. If you have some fresh lavender handy, crush a handful of the flower heads into the soda first. But sometimes you'll want a deeper clean. A cupful of vinegar in a large bucket of water will remove the film of grease and dirt that can build up on carpets. Take care to test the carpet first to check if it is colourfast: opt for a patch in the corner and leave overnight before applying to the whole carpet. Apply with a soft brush dipped in the weak vinegar solution.

Wooden floors and lino can be easier to keep clean, but they are particularly sensitive to footwear. Remove black heel marks from lino or wooden floors by rubbing with a cloth moistened with white spirits. Silver sand (available from your local gardening shop) brushed over wooden floors helps remove a build-up of grease. Scratches on wooden floors can be disguised by gently scuffing the problem area with wire wool before rubbing with floor wax coloured with brown shoe polish to blend it with the rest of the floor.

Remember that your hoover can do more than just clean floors. To clean dust from radiators, hang a damp cloth behind the radiator and, using the blower end of your hoover, blow the dust and dirt into the damp cloth. To deal with dents from heavy furniture, melt an ice cube in the dent, allow to dry fully and then hoover the spot to fluff up. You can even use your hoover to locate small items dropped and potentially lost on the floor, such as a ring or beads from jewellery. Simply place an old pop-sock or the leg of a pair of nylon tights over the nozzle of the hoover and allow the suction to create a little net out of the nylon to capture your precious items.

It's the Little Things...
"Add a few drops of essential oils to the filter in your vacuum cleaner to scent the room as you clean."
Theresa Storey, Limerick

Dealing with Carpet Stains

A great product for spot cleaning carpets or upholstery is Lifter 1 carpet stain remover, available in a spray can from most auto-repair shops. If you want to make your own shampoo for dealing with stains, mix up a solution of 150ml (¼ pint) of white vinegar with a teaspoon each of borax and salt. Soak a clean cloth in this solution and use to lightly rub the stain, and then soak the area with clean water after the stain is removed and allow to dry.

Reacting to spillages quickly helps deter stains from settling in. If you spill red wine on a carpet, dab the liquid with an absorbant cloth to remove the surface liquid and then pour salt generously onto the stain. If you act quickly enough, the salt will absorb most or all of the wine. Indeed, salt can be used to absorb many liquids, including blood, but you need to be fast. Red wine stains can also be removed with bicarbonate of soda. Just rub in the soda, allow the area to dry and then hoover it up. White wine stains can be lifted by pouring on one part vinegar mixed with four parts water and blotting up. To remove fresh grease spots from rugs and carpets, rub the spot with a generous helping of bicarbonate of soda, leave to absorb the grease overnight and then hoover or sweep up the soda the next day. Salt is also great for removing soot from a carpet. Cover the offending material liberally with salt and then both salt and soot can be simply swept or hoovered up.

Raw potato can be a handy aid in shifting tricky stains from carpets or rugs. Lay raw potato slices over mud marks to help move them, while ink stains can be removed by scraping raw potatoes and pressing over the ink spot. Sop it up and add another layer until the stain is eliminated.

More problematic than a stain is a cigarette burn, but you can disguise small burn holes by squeezing a little glue into the hole and filling with bits of pile plucked from the carpet. Allow to dry fully before gently pressing the pile to secure.

Upholstery & Curtains

'Well-loved' doesn't have to be a euphemism for well-worn when it comes to soft furnishings. You'll be amazed what a hot steam iron held for a few seconds above the arms of sofas and chairs can do in terms of refreshing flattened upholstery. Small dents in furniture can be steamed out using a steam iron or a regular iron and a damp cloth, but take care with delicate fabrics. Any loose furniture covers removed to be washed should be replaced while still damp so they stretch to fit.

Heavy velvet curtains are a warm and cosy addition to a room but they can get very dusty. It's worth taking them down every couple of months and airing them one at a time in the tumble drier for ten minutes each. They come out fresh and clean and the practice helps to bring up the pile on the velvet.

It's no surprise, given the damp air in many Irish households, that many of us struggle with mildew. If your curtains suffer from this particular challenge, you'll need to wash them regularly. Adding 150ml (¼ pint) of lavender-infused vinegar to the water when washing and another cup when rinsing will help lift the mould and keep it from building up again. You may want to rub heavy stains with a mixture of salt and lemon juice first.

If you have children or elderly people in the household, or anyone whose independent mobility might be compromised, it is a good idea to fire-proof curtains and rugs each time they are washed. It is easier than it sounds and is safe for the fabric, so no need to spot check in advance. Thoroughly dissolve 140g (5oz) of borax and 110g (4oz) of boric acid in 2 litres (4 pints) of hot water and immerse the pre-washed curtains or rugs. Wring them out before drying as normal. Curtains can be spun-dried or wrung and ironed, depending on the fabric, while rugs should ideally be hung out on a clothes line.

Making & Hanging Curtains

When making gathered curtains, fabric should be measured to be about 1½ times as wide as the width you're covering, or up to three times as wide if the fabric is very fine.

When putting curtains onto a metal rod, slip a plastic freezer bag over the metal end first to protect the curtain material from snagging and help it slip on easily.

It's a good idea to let curtains hang for a few days before the final hemming as they may stretch after hanging. If your curtains should shrink and you're lucky enough to have a pelmet or 'cornice board' (a framework placed above a window to conceal curtain fixtures), use a deeper set of hooks under the pelmet to drop the curtains down. Alternatively you could stitch a false top hem and use the regular hooks.

Consider insulating a room from drafts by lining your curtains with a plain coloured shower curtain using curtain hooks.

Walls & Ceilings

Sugar soap is a great aid in lifting the build-up of grease and smoke stains from painted walls and ceilings, especially in problem areas like kitchens and living rooms. Taking the time to wash your walls and ceilings at least once a year will pay off with the subtle lift that a bright clean space gives to its inhabitants.

The trick of course is not to let the little stains build up either, which is easier said than done in a family household, especially with small, sticky-fingered, pencil-happy children on the loose! Quick-fix tips for dealing with everyday stains include dabbing fingermarks with white bread and rubbing greasy spots with fine steel wool and washing-up liquid.

Marks from pens, markers and crayons can be tackled too. The green skin of a cucumber applied with care and patience can lift these with surprising results, or try WD-40 for a more immediate effect on crayon marks (also great for stubborn sticky labels, which can be cleared off with a plastic scraper once softened). You may be left with a little grease mark but nothing that can't be shifted with soap and water. If you don't have a spray can of the stuff handy, an alternative is to soften the crayon with a hairdryer: the heated crayon will be wiped off easily.

The damp atmosphere of a bathroom and sometimes even the kitchen can cause mildew or mould to form on the walls. Keeping the room well-ventilated helps to allow the excess moisture to escape, as does wiping down regularly with full strength vinegar. To banish stubborn black spots, dab with a paste of one part lemon juice to one part baking powder, leave for a couple of hours to work its magic and then rinse off. Vanish Oxi Action Crystal White Powder is a reliable shop-bought solution for mould – leave overnight for best results.

It's the Little Things...
"To save library shelves from mould, sprinkle oil of lavender sparingly through the bookcase."
Annascaul Guild Members, Kerry

Cut Down on Commercial Cleaners

BICARBONATE OF SODA is a mild alkali that is useful for neutralising acidic stains. It works well as a gentle abrasive cleaner on a damp cloth and is also a natural deodoriser, making it ideal for cleaning everything from fridges and ovens to china and stainless steel.

BORAX softens water and helps breaks down grease in sinks and drains. Always use protective gloves.

HOUSEHOLD AMMONIA is useful for glass surfaces and ceramic tiles: dilute with water and be sure to wear rubber gloves.

LEMON JUICE can be used to sterilise chopping boards and to lift limescale, rust and other stains from plastic worktops, and to buff up tarnished brass or copper.

METHYLATED SPIRIT is good on glass surfaces and ceramic tiles, but always take care with this flammable and poisonous substance.

RAW POTATOES can have many uses around the house, from lifting certain stains, such as ink, and shifting rust from cast iron pots to cleaning windows and even keeping your car windows fog-free.

SALT is great for shifting all sorts of stains, including blood, red wine, sweat and fruit stains (see p35-6). It's also handy for reacting to oven spills: covering the spilt liquid generously with table salt before it dries in will allow you to wipe away the salt and spillage once cooled.

VINEGAR can be used either neat to cut through grease, in a dilute solution with water to remove hard water deposits or in a paste mixed with borax and water for buffing taps.

WASHING SODA softens water and breaks down grease. Dissolve in hot water to clean hard floors, cooker hoods, extractor fans and drains. Wear protective gloves and do not confuse with soda crystals which can react with some substances, such as aluminium, to cause noxious fumes.

WHITE SPIRITS can be used to clean picture frames and mirrors as well as to gently remove built-up layers of wax polish and to dissolve rust spots on acrylic sinks and bathtubs.

Laundry

In an ideal world, our experience of doing the laundry would be epitomised by clothes lines of dazzling whites blowing in the breeze on a sunny day, and neatly stacked, perfectly pressed, colour-coded piles of clothes, each garment as vibrant as on the day it was bought. Instead we are more likely to associate it with the biting cold of taking the still-wet washing in off the line on a bitterly cold day as it's about to hail or rain, and piles of un-ironed clothes collecting creases in a musty corner of the house. It doesn't have to be this way, we promise.

Back in the Day…

"I have done many crafts in my time and still do, but my late mother Julie Casey was the best woman I have ever seen to turn the collar on a man's shirt. She would neatly rip the stitching with the little sharp scissors she kept hidden in her apron pocket, take the collar right off, turn it over and hand-sew it back in place with strong thread. A new lease of life to dad's shirts."

Betty Gorman, Laois

Maintaining Clothes

Before washing, take the time to fix up any items that need mending; the old adage about a stitch in time is never truer than when you are about to put a garment through the physical demands of a washing and drying cycle. You may, however, want to make an exception with dirty socks that need a little darning, and choose to wash these first!

Threading a needle can be a challenge, especially as we get older. It helps to hold both needle and thread over a white surface for easier vision, and you could also spray the thread with a little hairspray to stiffen it. When stitching tough fabric such as denim jeans, turn the needle through a cake of soap first. For particularly tough material, rub the material itself with candle wax or cooking paraffin.

A stuck zip can be eased by running a soft lead pencil over it several times to lubricate it. Runaway buttons can be resewn with dental floss for extra security (especially handy for children's clothes). If you'd rather use regular thread, you can protect against buttons dropping off by dabbing a little clear nail varnish over the thread to secure it in place.

Wonderweb hemming tape is very handy for turning up children's trousers but it can be trickier to remove it thoroughly when you want to let the hem out again. The tape can be removed easily enough by gently pulling off but the remaining residue that's left behind can be an irritant. Simply place some brown paper over the residue and press with an iron. The scratchy residue will transfer to the paper and be removed from the trousers. After dropping a stitched hemline, on the other hand, you can despatch the little thread holes left in the material by ironing over a vinegar-dampened cloth.

Washing

Like it or loathe it, laundry needs to be done regularly, especially in a family household. The longer clothes are allowed to remain dirty, the more time, washing powder and labour will be required to get them clean. Having said that, try not to over-wash or dry clean clothes too frequently. Even the gentlest cleaning can take its toll on fabrics and you'll simply wear them out faster. Instead, try airing on the line or remove odours such as stale cigarette smoke by steaming clothes overnight above a bathtub filled with hot water and 275ml (½ pint) of vinegar.

Letting it all pile up in a dirty laundry basket helps to make more of a chore of the job. To make it a more welcoming task to spend any time with, place a fabric softener sheet in the bottom of your laundry basket and change weekly, or simply shake some bicarbonate of soda into the basket to soak up the more offensive odours. Be systematic in your approach, washing all whites separately, as with woollens and coloured clothes. Wash bulkier items such as curtains, bed throws, blankets and duvets in summertime when they will dry more quickly, and try to start the process of washing when you'll be around long enough to see it through to drying.

Caring for... Your Washing Machine

Knowing how to and taking the time to look after an appliance is an important sign of a good housekeeper. To keep your washing machine running smoothly, be sure to keep the powder box clean. To remove soap scum and clean the grease and grime that build up in the hoses of your machine, periodically run an empty hot wash with nothing but a cupful of white distilled vinegar or some Swarfega (a brand of heavy-duty hand cleaner good for shifting grease).

Whites & Colours

The holy grail of colour care is to keep whites gleaming white and colour from running. It goes without saying that you should always separate white and coloured garments before washing them, and it is worth using washing powder or liquid specially formulated for coloured clothes. But our old friend vinegar is great both as a fabric brightener and colour fixer, and there are other everyday aids all around you.

There's nothing less attractive than off-grey underwear. Bleach is obviously an effective way of whitening your whites, especially for ensuring crisp white linen or cotton tablecloths, but it's not so friendly to delicate fabrics. You can halve the amount of bleach needed by adding a half cup of bicarbonate of soda to top-loading machines or half that again to front-loaders. To whiten greys, soaking in water with a dissolved dishwasher tablet for about an hour can be effective. Alternatively, add half a cup of white vinegar to the rinse cycle after washing clothes. Adding half a cup of lemon juice to the rinse cycle of a medium load of whites will lightly bleach them. This technique is especially effective on clothes that are to be hung out to dry on the line. For badly discoloured socks or dingy tea towels, try boiling them in a pot of water with a few slices of lemon or a cupful of vinegar and then leave to soak overnight. Alternatively, soaking in warm water and bicarbonate of soda will also help to shift stains.

Remember too that a little blue will help whites to look whiter, which is why people once used a blue bag to keep the whites white – so that old blue blanket is good to go into a white wash, although maybe not your new blue jeans.

When washing intense colours such as brand-new, bright reds, soak the fabric in vinegar before washing (taking care to rinse thoroughly in clean water before drying). This will stop them bleeding onto other items. To prevent colours in delicates from running, dissolve salt in hot water and pre-soak before washing. Adding either a teaspoon of salt or half a cupful of vinegar to the last rinse of a wash will help to brighten up colours, and remove the soap residue that makes black clothes look dull. Always wash jeans inside out, and the first wash should be detergent-free to help fix the colour.

Back in the Day…

"In my mother's time when all the washing was done by hand, starch would be added to the final rinse. As well as helping to give a crisply pressed look to clothes when ironing, this also made the next wash day's tasks that bit easier. As the clothes were being washed, the starch came out of the clothes taking the surface dirt with it."
Jackie Slattery, Clare

Washing Woollens

Aran sweaters will wash like new in a mild hand wash of soda crystals. If there are still some lingering odours, a rinse in equal parts water and vinegar should freshen things up. This will also help to fluff up the wool nicely.

If you accidentally shrink a woollen jumper, all is not lost. Soak it overnight in a solution of six tablespoons of vinegar to 500ml (1 pint) of water and you can pull it back into shape the following day.

To make woollen garments look as good as new, wash by hand or on the woollen cycle and dry flat. Then cover the garment with two layers of greaseproof paper and press with a hot iron.

To prevent an angora sweater from shedding (a particular problem when wearing dark clothes), wrap it in a plastic bag and place it in the freezer for several hours before wearing.

Looking after Leather

Use a waterproof and stain-protector spray on suede and fine leather, and polish all leathers regularly. You can make your own leather softener by combining equal parts hot lavender vinegar with olive oil. Blend well and buff on with a soft cloth. If you're more concerned with polishing the leather, spray with undiluted lavender vinegar and polish off with a soft duster. Deal with small spots of dirt on glossy leather by dabbing with a damp sponge, while scuff marks can be shifted with a shoe polish of the correct colour. Ink stains can be lifted by spraying with hair spray and wiping off with a clean cloth. (See p26 for more tips.)

Shifting Stains: an A–Z

The trick is to act fast: a fresh stain is easier to shift than one that has settled in. But acting fast doesn't mean tossing it in the washing machine – the detergent may help the stain to set and make it harder to lift later. (Baby wipes are a good all-rounder stain remover, or see more suggestions below.) For non-washable stains, get thee to the dry-cleaner as soon as you can, and don't forget to tell them what the stain is. For washable fabrics, you'll need to work on the stain before washing, either with a commercial stain remover or by one of the more traditional methods suggested below. Remember, always work from the edge of the stain inwards to prevent it from spreading further. Vinegar is a powerful aid for all sorts of stains, from tea and coffee to fruit and grass. Mixed into a paste with bicarbonate of soda, it can tackle build up on shirt cuffs and collars – though of course the old-fashioned practice of turning collars is an even defter solution.

ACIDS: Rinse thoroughly in cold water before neutralising with a paste of bicarbonate of soda and water.

BLOOD: Rub fresh stains with a little soda water or saliva on a piece of tissue, or scrub with salt, rinse and repeat. For dried blood stains, work in a paste of water and bicarbonate of soda, allow to dry and brush off. Whites can be steeped in salt and warm water.

CHEWING GUM: Chewing gum is easier to prise off once frozen. Press an ice cube wrapped in a plastic bag against it so that you can crack the gum off and remove any residue by ironing with brown paper (as with wax, below).

CHOCOLATE: Remove any excess chocolate and soak the area with soda water or biological detergent. Whites can be dabbed with a little bleach.

EGG: Rinse well in cold water and then wash thoroughly with hot water and soap.

GRASS: Dab hydrogen peroxide directly onto the stain and wash as normal.

GREASE & OIL: Douse with salt and leave it to work for an hour before shaking off and rinsing well in warm, lightly salted water. For delicate suede items, brush the stain gently with a toothbrush dipped in vinegar.

HAIR DYE: Zap the spot with some hair spray as soon as possible, and then simply wash as normal – great for ink stains too (see below).

INK STAINS: If you can treat immediately, dab with methylated spirit or hairspray (especially for leather). Otherwise, douse with salt (as with grease stains, above) or soak in milk for an hour, dab with a vinegar-cornflour paste, allow to dry and wash as normal.

LIPSTICK: Scrub with white non-gel toothpaste, rinse and repeat if necessary. Good for ballpoint pen marks too.

MILDEW: Soak in milk or buttermilk for 48 hours and wash as normal.

MOULD: Rub a paste of lemon juice and salt into the stain, leave for an hour, rinse well and wash as normal. Repeat if necessary but if the stains persist, they may need a dry clean to shift them.

PAINT: Rub with a cloth doused in white spirits to lift paint or polish.

PERSPIRATION: Crush an aspirin tablet and mix in a little warm water. Soak the stain with this solution for a couple of hours before washing. Watered down lemon juice or undiluted vinegar can be sponged or sprayed on before washing – both will shift odours and lift deodorant stains too.

POLLEN: Take care not to rub in. Instead, a little sellotape over the pollen should lift it. In the case of lily pollen, the best way to get rid of it is by rubbing with another part of the same garment. Do not be tempted to use a damp cloth or different textured cloth.

RUST STAINS: A combination of salt and either lemon juice or vinegar helps banish rust stains. Allow to dry (in the sunshine, in the case of whites) before washing.

SCORCH MARKS: Scrub with raw onion and leave for a few hours before washing. Or rub lightly with a silver coin for serious scorches. Alternatively, cornflour can be applied to the dampened mark, allowed to dry and brushed away.

TAR: Apply a few drops of neat vinegar onto the stain and wash as normal.

WAX: Lay a brown paper bag over the wax stain and gently melt it with a medium-warm iron. Keep moving the bag around to absorb the wax. A soft tea towel can be used in place of the paper.

WINE: Pour white wine vinegar over red wine stains and wash immediately. Alternatively, just-boiled water poured through the stained fabric will help to lift it – take care not to burn yourself.

Drying

To tumble dry or not to tumble dry: that is the question. The answer is a somewhat personal choice and will depend on factors such as affordability (it ain't cheap), delicacy of fabrics (it ain't gentle) and availability of alternatives such as sunny washing lines, steaming radiators or space for a clothes horse. There are many who would never tumble dry anything but towels and sheets and others who draw the line at precious underwear. Certainly you should take care with heat-sensitive synthetic items or impressionable natural fabrics which might lose shape, and err on the side of too short a cycle rather than too long. Throwing a clean, dry bath towel into the dryer will help to absorb moisture, allowing clothes to dry faster.

Speaking of towels, if you ever wondered how to dry your bath towels so that they're lovely and fluffy again, the answer is tennis balls. Really! Throw them in the dryer with your towels and let them work their magic. But the truth is that it's more about the wash than the dry for towels. To lift all built-up residue, avoid fabric softeners, don't overfill the washer and opt for a vinegar rinse before the final rinse. Likewise, blankets will come out all fluffy and soft if a splash of white spirits is added to final rinse.

If you don't own a tumble dryer, you may be more dependent on a good drying day and may find yourself prone to leaving clothes sitting in the washer while waiting for the weather to turn. Keeping the door closed helps to keep them fresh, but if they do start to smell a little you may need to rewash – add a few tablespoons of ammonia to help shift the smell. Take care when hanging clothes not to mark or stretch the garment. Some natural fabrics such as linen and wool are best dried flat (on the grass outdoors or on a towel indoors) while others are better dried on a hanger rather than pegged to the line.

Caring for...Your Tumble Dryer

Clean the lint filter regularly, and wipe down the machine inside and out on a regular basis. Try not to open the door while it's operating but keep it open when off. Don't overfill your dryer (two thirds full is optimum) and take particular care with synthetic duvets, which can potentially melt if dried in an overloaded drum. Always loosen clothes before loading and dry similar fabrics together.

Ironing

We all have our quirks. For some of us, ironing is a form of meditation; for others, a kind of slow, never-ending torture. Whether you choose to iron your undies is your own call, and good drying techniques (such as shaking the garment well before hanging or tumble drying) can help to cut down on the necessary pressing. But there's no denying the pleasure of slipping between freshly washed, crinkle-free linen sheets.

A quick iron can be a great way to revive clothes without washing them, especially if you use a little starch to crisp-up tired fabric. You can make up your own home-made laundry starch by dissolving a tablespoon of cornstarch in a pint of cold water. Dispense from a spray bottle, shaking well before use. Adding a drop of perfume to your starch spray will refresh stale odours. Musky cotton can be sprinkled with white distilled vinegar before ironing. You don't need starch to smarten up all clothes, however: for a sharper crease in trousers, turn inside out, rub along the inside of the crease with a dry piece of soap, turn back out and press.

Take the time to fold items properly before putting away. Keep sets of bed linen together when storing; if you put each folded set inside one of the pillow cases, they will be easier to find on another day.

> " To prevent tights from getting tangled on the line on breezy days, drop a coin down each leg. "
> Bernie McAndrew, Mayo

Iron a Shirt

1. Aim to remove most creases before your shirt or trousers hit the ironing board, and be very particular about which creases you add to the finished garment.

2. You'll get a much smoother finish if you iron clothes from damp rather than bone dry. And it will take less elbow grease too, which is always welcome.

3. If you won't be ironing straight away, shake out the shirt well to smooth out creases, place it on a hanger and button it right up to encourage it to dry in shape.

4. Always check the care instructions on any garment, but if they are not there, pay attention at the very least to the fabric and be sure to set your iron to the correct temperature. Err on the side of caution to avoid burning the fabric.

5. Spray cotton shirts with starch before ironing. Linen items will iron up lovely and crisp if you pop them in the freezer for fifteen minutes first.

6. If you are ironing nylon, shake some talcum powder on the end of the ironing board. Slide the iron through the talcum powder to help it slide over the garments without sticking.

7. Approach a shirt in parts, pressing the unbuttoned collar first (inwards towards the centre to avoid the collar points from crumpling), then the upper shoulders (one side at a time and using the narrower end of your board to gain access), and then the front and back individually (working from the bottom up).

8. To tackle the row of buttons, fold a towel into several thicknesses, lay the shirt button-side down on the towel and iron it from the inside. This is particularly important if the shirt doesn't open fully, in order to avoid marking the back of the shirt.

9. To press the sleeves and cuffs, lay each sleeve out carefully, smoothing it out with your hands using the bottom seam as a guide. Use the method above to iron around the button on the cuff, and then open the cuff and press it from the inside.

10. Be sure to capture all that hard work by hanging your shirt properly, with the top button closed and in a wardrobe with enough space to ensure it doesn't pick up any new creases. For that professional finish, you could cover it with plastic or tissue paper.

Caring for... Your Iron

An iron's base should be kept smooth, clean and shiny so that it will not harm any fabric, but this can take a bit of maintenance. For a quick clean, run the hot iron over a piece of tin foil. To banish brown scorch marks, rub with a paste of vinegar and bicarbonate of soda or a warmed up solution of half vinegar, half salt. Clean thoroughly with a wet cloth. A build-up of starch can produce a sticky base; to remove stickiness, iron over salt scattered on thick paper. If your iron is not running smoothly, try wrapping some soap in cotton fabric and rub the hot iron over it several times.

A steam iron should be cleaned regularly to avoid a build-up of mineral deposits: simply fill with equal parts water and vinegar, or water with a little detergent. Set the thermostat to full, allow to steam in an upright position until the liquid is evaporated, and rinse thoroughly with cold water.

Insulating your ironing board with a layer of tin foil beneath the cover will help retain the heat and allow your iron to work more efficiently – but take care not to burn the fabric with the increased heat.

Back in the Day...

"My mother was born in the early 1920s and I in the 1950s. I remember when my mother recycled flour bags with 'Ranks Flour' stamped on them. These were cloth bags which contained four stone of flour. She would rip the stitching on each bag until it opened up to a white square of cloth. When she had four bags collected she would wash them and boil them until they were white. Then she would sew the four pieces together using the 'run and fell seam' stitch to make a sheet for the bed.

All clothes and materials were recycled. Quilts were made from old discarded clothes stitched together in a patchwork style and lined with the home-made sheets. Coats and jackets were 'turned' and remade to suit a younger member of the family. Shirt collars that were worn were taken off, turned around and sewn back on again for further wear. Aprons were made from discarded dresses. All woollen jumpers were hand-knitted. Socks were knitted and the heels darned when they were worn. My grandmother knit a pair of socks every night, I am told. Old woollen garments were ripped up to knit smaller children's cardigans and jumpers. When eventually a garment got too shabby for further use, the buttons and zips were cut off and kept to help in the making up of new garments.

When, in later years, those cloth flour bags were replaced by paper, I used the inner layer of these brown paper bags to cover school books. The brown paper from farm feedstuff bags was also ironed out and used to cover the school books. (My children remind me now that the books carried the odour of the feedstuffs for several days!) Leftover and end of roll wallpaper were used also, making the book covers very colourful and varied.

Nothing was wasted that could be used in any way – something we could all learn from today."

Peg Prendeville, Limerick

Bathroom

It's where you meet yourself first thing in the morning and last thing at night, and it's where women in particular love to retreat for some special 'me time'. The bathroom should be a welcoming place, so if it reproaches you with grubby grouting and creeping mildew every time you're in there, then you need to take back control. Set aside a time (and preferably allocate a volunteer) to look after a weekly clean but don't let the less frequent jobs be put on the long finger. There's nothing that can spoil a leisurely bath like worrying about the mildew on the ceiling.

Speaking of leisurely baths, treat yourself to some affordable luxuries. Invest in an oil burner and some tea light candles, and handpick a selection of essential oils which you can either burn or drop directly into the bathwater. Lavender is great for unwinding while rose and geranium are more sensual. Piles of fluffy towels (see p36 for tips) and bars of natural hand-made soaps (often available at farmers' markets around the country) will all add to the ambiance, as will maintaining some bathroom-friendly plants for extra colour.

Regular Cleaning

These are the little jobs that we need to do every week or even every day in the bathroom to keep the place pretty and sparkling and not let dirt or bacteria build up. But who said you should do it all by yourself, especially if you have a large family and most especially if you have boys with wandering aims? (A wine cork in the toilet bowl can be a good target practice for little ones.) Train them up young – both to make as little mess as possible and to clean up what messes they do make!

SINKS & BATHS

Keep a little piece of net curtain in your bathroom and use it after washing your hands to wash down the basin with whatever residue of soap remains – you'll have an instant shine.

For cleaning sinks and taps, rubbing with cucumber will give three-fold benefits: by helping to clean the area, by bringing back the shine lost under years of tarnish and by being easy on your hands. Hard lime deposits around taps can be softened for easy removal by covering with vinegar-soaked paper towels. Leave the paper towels on for one hour cleaning. It leaves chrome clean and shiny.

General bath stains can be removed with a salt-covered piece of lemon. To shift scum and dirt from your bath, mix a spray bottle up with one part baby oil to four parts water. Spray onto the problem section and wipe off with a sponge before finishing with a disinfectant cleaner. Dishwasher detergent gel is also effective: leave for 15 minutes and rinse thoroughly to avoid slipperiness.

If you have marks from dripping taps, try rubbing with either a paste of lemon juice and salt or scrubbing with a toothbrush dipped in cream of tartar and peroxide. Rinse thoroughly after either treatment.

SHOWERS & TILES

Keep a squidgy window-wiper beside the shower and when finished showering, clean down the glass immediately. Wipe down the shower door with a little shower gel and use the window-wiper to remove surface water and guarantee a lovely clear door. This prevents the glass from getting stained and discoloured and saves you having to scrub it later.

WD-40 is a good replacement for those expensive cleaners for shower stalls and doors. It makes them sparkle, so give it a try. For an economical route to sparkling bathroom tiles, sprinkle a little boric acid onto the tiles before washing. A home-made scouring mix made up of a paste of bicarbonate of soda with bleach and applied with a nylon pad will remove stubborn scum from shower tiles.

A clogged shower-head should be dismantled (unscrew it to remove the rubber washer) and the pieces soaked in a bowl of vinegar for two to three hours. Alternatively place the dismantled head in a pot filled with equal parts vinegar and water, bring to a boil, then simmer for five minutes. Rinse in hot water, allow to dry and clean off any sediment with a stiff brush before reassembling to keep the water flowing freely.

TOILETS

To clear the scale in the lavatory, bale out the water to below the line of deposit. Make up a mixture of domestic borax and vinegar in equal quantities. Spread the mixture on the deposits and leave for two to three hours. Brush off the sediment with a stiff brush. Treat all hard water deposits on bathroom fittings as necessary. If you've ever done the cola test on an old penny then you'll know how effective it is in cutting through the most persistent dirt. Toilet bowls also come up shiny when cleaned with old, flat Coke or Pepsi. Simply leave overnight to dissolve limescale.

Mind the Pennies...

Well-maintained bathroom utensils will yield a longer lifespan. Disinfect toothbrushes by soaking in white vinegar every fortnight. Slimy sponges can be revived by soaking in diluted vinegar for an hour (but be sure to rinse thoroughly afterwards).

Deeper Cleaning

There are certain jobs that you won't want to be doing on a weekly basis, but that are worth working into your monthly or quarterly cleaning schedule.

A sparkling bathroom can be really let down by grubby grouting between tiles. Apply bleach on an old toothbrush to clean grouts, and rinse thoroughly. Spraying with oven cleaner is another good way to brighten them up. If your grouts have a build-up of bathroom mildew, dilute 150ml (¼ pint) of bleach in three litres (6 pints) of water. Apply to the grout with a toothbrush, scrub to lift the mildew and rinse well.

Rub mildewed shower curtains with bicarbonate of soda or lemon juice. To prevent mildew forming again, soak in salted water before re-hanging. To wash shower curtains, wash with warm water and a half cup each of detergent and baking soda, but add two large bath towels to the washing drum with the curtains. Allow to run through the entire wash cycle and then add a cup of vinegar to the rinse. Do not spin dry or wash the vinegar out but hang immediately and allow to drip dry for a wrinkle-free curtain.

To help get rid of superficial bathroom smells, an effective alternative to air fresheners is striking a regular match. Sometimes the problem goes deeper, however. Smelly drains can be dealt with by boiling up a glassful of vinegar and pouring directly into the drain. Leave for ten minutes to work its effects before using the drain.

For a home-made drain cleaner, make up a solution of 200ml (7fl oz) of vinegar with 75g (3oz) of bicarbonate of soda. Pour directly into the drain, leave for ten minutes and run clean hot water down the drain to clear the grease and debris. Waste-pipe blockages can be freed by flushing with a strong soda solution. In stubborn cases, use soda crystals directly. Flush crystals down the toilet to keep it fresh and free from blockages.

Mirrors & Windows

Never use soap when cleaning windows or mirrors. A home-made window cleaner is more effective than most commercial versions, and it's certainly cheaper. For sparkling streak-free clean windows, mix two tablespoons of vinegar into a basin of warm water. Wring out a piece of chamois leather in the solution and rub over the windows. Allow to dry before buffing to a brilliant shine with crumpled newspaper – but be sure to wear rubber gloves as the newspaper will blacken your hands. For a quick clean, simply soak a piece of newspaper in clean water, squeeze it out and rub the window, and then use another dry piece of newspaper to dry the window, as above.

Streaks can sometimes be caused by washing windows in the sunshine, which dries them very quickly. Waiting until they are in the shade helps, but also consider wiping the inside vertically and the outside horizontally. This way if streaks do appear you will at least know which side they are on.

A few drops of methylated spirit on a damp cloth will give a beautiful depth and sparkle to mirrors. Polish afterwards with a soft dry cloth. To prevent shaving mirrors from steaming up, rub with a piece of cucumber or with shaving foam and polish off. For a lint-free look for bathroom mirrors, you can clean them with white wine and buff up with coffee filter paper.

Mind the Pennies...

"Use up leftover pieces of soap by mashing them up with a little glycerine and warm water to make a liquid soap that is both gentle and economical."
Ballyroan Guild Members, Laois

Bedroom

A well-maintained bedroom is a place of refuge from the rest of the world, somewhere you look forward to retreating to rather than another battleground with that never-ending list of things to do. Aside from the basics of changing linen regularly and keeping the place clean and tidy, there are little extras which you will want to do every once in a while.

Pillows & Mattresses

Fibre or foam-filled pillows can be washed in your washing machine. To keep their shape while washing, take eight large safety pins: use one of these in each of the four corners to pin together the cover and filling and place the other four pins halfway between each of the corners. Note that this is not suitable for feather pillows.

Mattresses should be turned on a regular basis to ensure that they don't develop a hollow where you lie every night. This should be done at least twice a year, but doing it every two or three months will stretch the lifespan of your mattress even further. Don't forget to alternate turning it over (so the underside is up) and around (so the head end is at the feet end). For this reason, turning it four times a year makes for good practice. Pin a little card to either end of the mattress with the allocated months for turning, say February (right side up) and May (upside down) on one end, and November (right side up) and August (upside down) on the other. This way, when changing sheets, your memory will be jogged to do the job and you won't be confused as to which way to turn.

Remember that mattresses can be very heavy, so be sure to enlist the help of someone else for this particular chore. If it's a sunny day, a few hours outside in the back garden is a great way to chase away any bed mites that might have set up home in your mattress. Take the opportunity to hoover under the bed and in those hard to reach corners while turning your mattress, and air the room well to banish any mites you may have disturbed.

Unwanted Visitors: Moths & Mites

Once you have an infestation of moths you'll know all about it, but you can do several things to prevent them from making your house their home. Moths love shady places and particularly like dark, undisturbed corners where they can lay their eggs in peace. Look out for the warning signs of little eggs (the shape of a grain of rice and the shimmery colour of moths). Hoover carpets regularly and thoroughly, especially in danger areas such as under beds and radiators and at the corner base of long curtains.

Do a regular clearout of drawers and wardrobes, and store winter woollens in protective plastic covering (moths love wool). Scatter cloves or cinnamon sticks among the articles contained in boxes and drawers. They are as effective as naphtha balls and more pleasant to use. Or lay some sheets of moth deterrent down; these can be picked up at your hardware store and are very effective. If you are unlucky enough to get an infestation, don't hope they'll go away. They won't – or at least not unless you wash and clean everything thoroughly, including the inside of each wardrobe and all of its belongings.

Regular cleaning is also important for asthma sufferers, who can be sensitive to dust mites as well as to the dust itself. Mites love warm, humid places, so keeping bedrooms cool will help, as will airing well – particularly after hoovering carpets, when the little creatures will become airborne. Keeping pets out of bedrooms is important too as dust mites feed off human and animal skin particles. Mites don't spread disease, however, and are harmless enough except to asthma sufferers.

Kitchen

You want your kitchen to be a source of nourishment and pleasure, not hazards and worry. Most good kitchen practice comes down to good sense, literally: your eyes and nose will tell you much, as long as you take the time to pay attention. Good daily habits go a long way to cutting down work in the long run, but there are things which it is worth reminding yourself to do on a regular basis, such as changing or washing dishcloths, scrubbing oven tops and keeping drains clear. Once you have the basics of hygiene and cleanliness sorted, you'll want to stock your kitchen well, both in terms of equipment and fall-back foods. Organisation is key, as is taking care to make the most of whatever you spend your money on, whether that is fresh food or good knives.

A Wipe in Time…

Baked-on grease takes considerable time and effort to remove. Make life easier for yourself and wipe over the top of the cooker after every cooking session to save you serious cleaning chores down the line. A touch of polish on your kitchen worktops and table makes them easier to wipe clean every time, stopping food particles from getting caught in nicks and grooves.

To prevent mould and mildew from forming in breadbins and fridges, wipe them out with vinegar. The acid in the vinegar effectively kills the mildew fungus. Rubbing chopping boards down regularly with full strength vinegar cuts through grease, kills germs and gets rid of strong odours such as onion and garlic, as does dry mustard. Alternatively, scrub wooden chopping boards with a cut lemon sprinkled with salt for a gently abrasive cleanse.

A few tablespoons of washing soda dissolved in a litre of warm water and poured down the sink every week will prevent a build-up of grease and grime.

Kitchen Odours

Cleaning as you go will help prevent build-up of general odours, as will employing good practice in terms of food storage and rotation. And of course, while we don't like sniffy odours in a kitchen, there are certain unwanted visitors who love them, so best practice is important for peace of mind as well as making for a more pleasant ambiance.

Fridges in particular can be a source of bad smells – see opposite for some tips. Rinse out your rubbish bin regularly with a strong soda crystal solution and counteract unpleasant smells in summertime by sprinkling the clean, dry base with salt or bicarbonate of soda. Cat litter in the base of the bin will prevent odours building up in the first place.

The smell of boiled cauliflower can be less than pleasing, but odours can be reduced by boiling from cold water to which a teaspoon of sugar per head of cauliflower has been added. Alternatively, adding a little milk will reduce the smell and prevent discolouration. When cooking cabbage and broccoli as well as cauliflower, a little bread crust in the saucepan with these vegetables will prevent unpleasant odours, as will adding a bay leaf to the boiling water.

When something burns on a cooker, sprinkle salt on it immediately to prevent smells of burning. Chase away lingering cooking smells by simmering a teaspoon of ground cinnamon or ground cloves in 250ml (½ pint) of water for 15 minutes. Vanilla and orange peel are also pleasant and effective. An orange skin or peel burned over a gas flame will quickly rid the kitchen of cooking or other odours.

Fridge Odours

At one point or another, just about everyone will encounter a bad smell in the fridge. Frustratingly, it is not always simple to detect the source of the odour. Obnoxious odours can be attributed to many things such as spoilage, unclean refrigerator conditions or simply keeping very potent smelling products such as garlic or onions on hand. Best practice is to prevent smells developing in the first instance.

Meat is one of the main contributors to fridge odours. Raw meat should be used immediately or cooked within a day or two of purchase. If time is slipping away, cook it off and freeze for later use. Raw meat should be wrapped tightly and stored on the bottom shelf. Leaking blood or juices will not only create odour but can cross-contaminate other food.

Smelly ingredients such as blue cheese and raw onions should be kept to a minimum and used within a day or so. However, a halved onion can also absorb other smells but discard it after a day or so (likewise with a lemon). If leftover food will realistically not be consumed soon, bin it to avoid the containers getting pushed back to the rear of the fridge to grow mould and develop nasty odours that will taint your fresh food.

To clean a bad-smelling fridge, remove all foodstuffs, check all dates and discard any expired food. Dissolve half a cup of bicarbonate of soda in a sinkful of warm water and wash, rinse and thoroughly dry all parts of the fridge including drawers and shelves. An open box of bicarbonate of soda will neutralise fridge odours, but should be changed and discarded every three months: write the date on it before you put it in to remind you. Alternatively, place a small, uncovered bowl of either oats, used coffee grounds or charcoal (the kind used for potted plants) on a shelf in the fridge to help absorb some of the bad smells. Or you could try a little vanilla essence poured onto a piece of cotton wool and placed inside the refrigerator for a sweet-smelling counteraction to build-up of odours.

Caring for... Fridges and Freezers

To clean rubber seals on fridges and freezers, wipe down and scrub with an old toothbrush and some cheap toothpaste. Leave for 15 minutes and wipe off with a wet cloth. To cover up surface scratches on most fridges and freezers, try using the same colour enamel paint. This works really well and will last a long time. Stainless steel fridges and freezers shine up beautifully with a little baby oil.

Defrost your freezer or ice box on a regular basis. After defrosting, rub the inside with glycerine. Next time you have to defrost, you should find the ice will come away easily. Every couple of months, dust off the condenser coil at the back or base of a fridge to keep it running efficiently and clean out the drip tray inside the fridge.

For best practice, don't overcrowd a fridge but do keep your freezer as full as possible. The frozen items will help to keep the temperature down and save the freezer having to work so hard – saving on energy wastage and saving you money too. See How to... Use Your Freezer (p96) for tips on making the most of your freezer by using it for everything from leftover wine to home-made ice-packs.

Unwanted Visitors: Flies & Mice

To say goodbye to pesky fruit flies (the ones that always know when you have come back from shopping with fresh fruit!), fill a small glass halfway with cider vinegar and two drops of washing-up liquid and mix well. The flies will be drawn to the cup and will be banished forever.

The ancient Romans used parsley as a fly deterrent, so why don't you? Mint and basil work well too. Store your washed herbs on the kitchen windowsill in a glass with a little water, or better still grow a couple of plants. They will add to a pleasant ambiance, as well as being handy for your cooking and saving on waste and expense. Bunches of dried lavender make for pretty and efficient fly deterrents too.

Dealing with mice is no fun for anyone, but there are some useful tips. Mice are curious creatures, so pop the mouse trap into a brown paper bag. It'll make throwing it away that bit easier too. For a cheap and effective bait, try setting the trap with pumpkin seeds. Mice love them and the seed will not be easily removed by the mouse as long as you put it on firmly. If you want to make the pumpkin seed even more alluring, rub a little cheese, peanut butter or chocolate over the upper surface of the seed before setting the trigger on the trap. You can remove the smell of a dead mouse by cleaning the area thoroughly, wiping with either vinegar or bleach and placing a fabric softener sheet in the area to remove any lingering odours.

Kitchen Equipment & Appliances

Cooking can be so much more enjoyable – and so much easier – if you have the right kit to hand. Today there are any number of kitchen gadgets and appliances available for us to spend our money on but our mothers and grandmothers managed with a few well-cared for basics.

There is no point in buying expensive gadgets, even if they appear versatile, unless you are sure you will get plenty of use out of them. You may well decide to continue using your hand-held grater or the well-proven balloon whisk – and it would be hard to find more versatile items than a wooden spoon, a spatula and a good, sharp vegetable knife.

THE ESSENTIALS

A good knife is one of the most essential tools in the kitchen. Invest in a small paring knife, a large carving knife for meat (or an electric alternative) and a good strong cook's knife for chopping and slicing vegetables and raw meat. Choose good quality carbon steel or stainless steel. Remember that more accidents are caused by a blunt knife slipping than by use of a sharp knife, so invest in a sharpening steel and sharpen your knives regularly. Never throw a sharp knife into a washing-up bowl with other cutlery – to do so risks both cutting yourself and blunting the blade.

A selection of wooden spoons and measuring spoons is useful. Pick up some US measures as well if you have American cookbooks or recipe apps (a lot of websites for baking recipes are US-based).

Saucepans come in a wide variety of materials, from flowery patterned, heatproof glass to heavy enamelled iron. Keep in mind a few important facts when choosing, such as what type of cooker you use (solid fuel, gas or electric ceramic hob?) and how much you want to pay. A good choice is a mid-priced stainless-steel saucepan with a copper or aluminium base: these are hardwearing, easy to use and clean, and the base conducts the heat quickly throughout the pan.

Apart from the basics there are some specialised things that one cook will find essential and another will find completely useless. A big preserving pan is essential if you regularly make your own marmalade and jams in big quantities, while a fish kettle or an asparagus steamer will be essential for very few cooks. Pressure cookers and microwaves are either rarely used or essential equipment, depending on your own cooking practice: both are useful for making very quick stews, soups or stock without boiling away all the nutritional value. A slow cooker is ideal for cooking cheap, tough cuts of meat, whole chickens and ham joints and to make puddings. It is safe to leave unattended for several hours, freeing you up to do other things, and is very energy efficient.

Missing Equipment

Necessity is the mother of invention, and a little imagination can be very useful when you do not have the specialised tool called for in a recipe. A deep roasting tin filled with water serves well as a bain marie for an oven, while a heatproof saucer or some washed pebbles in the bottom of a saucepan of water does the same job as an expensive and bulky steamer. You can replace a missing rolling pin with a clean wine bottle or jam jar; remove the base from a well-washed empty salmon or tuna tin to double as a scone cutter and a poached egg ring; and small biscuit tins (such as butter biscuit or shortbread tins) when greased and lined can be used to make a sponge or fruit cake.

KITCHEN APPLIANCES

Kitchen appliances are worth buying well and looking after too. Grind a cup of rice in your coffee grinder to both sharpen the blades and clean while you're at it. Blenders and food processors can be hard to clean thoroughly, especially if you have been chopping meat, but processing some stale bread before washing up makes it considerably easier.

The simplest way to clean toasting and grilling machines after use is to unplug, cover the warm grill plate with a damp cloth and close the lid down. Leave it to steam away while you eat and then just wipe the softened residue clean, with no scrubbing needed.

Sometimes the smell of cooked food (and fish in particular) is difficult to remove from a microwave. To help shift smells and soften baked-on food splashes, add slices of lemon or orange to a bowl of water (or mix up a solution of three parts water to one part vinegar) and cook it for five or 10 minutes on the lowest heat setting. Wipe dry afterwards.

Caring for... Your Oven

Vinegar is great for budging baked-in grease. Combine with coarse salt for a stovetop scrub, or pour into a saucepan and place on the middle shelf of the oven, preheated to the highest setting. For a grease-splattered oven door, saturate with full strength vinegar and keep the door open for 15 minutes before wiping clean. For a very badly stained cooker top, make a paste of biological washing powder and water and leave for several hours or until the stains soften and can be scrubbed off with a plastic scrubber. Tackle stubborn spots with steel wool and bicarbonate of soda.

One simple habit will help to cut down on a build-up of oven grease and save on elbow grease. Dissolve two tablespoons of bicarbonate of soda in 570ml (1 pint) of boiling water, allow to cool and store in a screw-top jar or bottle. After using the oven, moisten a cloth with the solution and wipe the insides down while the oven is still warm. Allow to dry and leave the white marks which will appear. The next time you wipe down the oven after use, the burnt grease will come off easily.

For solid fuel stoves, you can easily clean sooty marks off the inside of the stove door by dipping an old damp cloth or sponge in the fine ash (avoiding any gritty bits) and wiping down. Clean the top of your solid fuel cooker with wax paper from bread wrapping.

Washing Up

Some cooks love to make a real mess, using every utensil they can get their hands on and letting everything pile up for the designated washer-upper to deal with later. Sound familiar? Of course, if that designated washer-upper is also the cook, you may prefer to work a little more efficiently.

While preparing food, clear up as you go. Anything that needs just a quick rinse should be dispatched immediately. Everything else should be stacked according to what is for the dishwasher and what must be washed by hand, and rinsing residue first will speed up the washing later. Try to rinse pans while still hot; they will be far easier to wash later. Take the opportunity to wash up and wipe down surfaces while waiting on something to cool or giving something in the oven another few minutes.

As well as a clean dishcloth (which should be changed or boiled on a regular basis to avoid a build-up of bacteria) and a good scrubbing brush, keep a little steel wool handy for tackling trickier items. To prevent steel wool from rusting, place it in a cupful of water with a little bicarbonate of soda after use. You might want to keep the soda handy too, especially if you suffer from hard water – a tablespoon added to the washing up will soften water and save on detergent. A little lemon peel in washing-up water acts as a rinse aid, and is handy for shifting persistent fishy odours.

Gleaming Sinks

Remember to never put grease or oil down your sink – besides blocking the drains eventually, it is bad for our water system. Instead keep an empty jar with a lid to fill with waste grease and oil and dispose of it in your general rubbish bin. Get into the good habit of wiping the sink down after every use. Doing so with a cut lemon will keep it gleaming and it also removes limescale from taps – you could dip it in a little salt if you need a gentle scrub. Rust marks can be removed from sinks by rubbing with lighter fluid on a rag.

SAUCEPANS & POTS

Fill burnt saucepans with a strong solution of salt and water, leave overnight and then bring slowly to the boil. The burnt food should come away easily. Salt is better for this than washing soda because soda is liable to make the saucepan burn again next time it is used. You can also clean burnt-on food from your saucepans with a sliced onion and a dessertspoon of salt. Leave overnight and the burnt food should come off without too much trouble.

For a heavy-duty cleaner, heat some cola in your dirty pan and see how it gleams. For aluminium pots and pans which have become stained (perhaps by steaming puddings), the acids released by boiling up some rhubarb will remove discolouration and the pans will come up brilliantly clean.

After mashing spuds, be sure to soak the potato masher and pan in cold water rather than hot. Save out-of-date credit or debit cards to use as scrapers for washing pots used for mash or porridge: they will do the job in seconds with just a few quick turns around the pot.

To lift rust from cast iron pots, rub with the cut side of half a potato dipped in washing-up liquid or scouring powder. Rinse well and grease with a little cooking oil on a paper towel. Rusted tin baking pans and cake tins can be given the potato treatment too. Washing these and other metal equipment while the oven is still warm allows you to dry them in the oven, which will help prevent rusting.

GLASSWARE

To get glasses sparkling, wash them first in hot soapy water, rinse in cold clear water and leave to dry. Vinegar added to the rinse water (about half a teaspoon to two litres or four pints) will give added sparkle. Glasses should be dried with a clean, dry linen cloth or a designated glass cloth.

Glasses stacked for drying can sometimes become wedged together. To separate without damaging or scratching them, fill the top glass with cold water and stand the outer glass in warm water. They should come apart easily.

Jam jars can be recycled for all sorts of handy uses, from shaking up dressings to storing roasted seeds or even serving up desserts. After washing, to get rid of glue residue from sticky labels simply wipe with baby oil. Eggshells can be used to clean glass bottles: break the shells into the bottle with a few drops of detergent and a drop of water, and shake vigorously. Likewise, rice is useful as a gentle abrasive.

DISHES & DELPH

Save yourself scrubbing that grungy casserole dish with the caked-on food. Simply fill with boiling water, add several tablespoons of salt and allow to soak until cooled, when everything should slide off easily. (Some swear by the addition of fabric

softener in place of the salt.)

Bicarbonate of soda on a soft cloth should shift stains from mugs and cups. For stubborn stains, scrub gently with equal parts salt (or baking powder) and vinegar. Rinse clean. Before storing seldom-used crockery or china, wash and dry thoroughly, stack together and wrap in clingfilm so that it is ready for immediate use without the need for re-washing.

Caring for... Your Dishwasher

Once a month, run your dishwasher on empty for a full cycle with just a cupful of vinegar added to the rinse compartment. This prevents hard deposits getting a head start, and it also prevents soap build-up and keeps it fresh from lingering smells. Your dishwasher will thank you with a spot-free rinse. Alternatively, pour four tablespoons of , bicarbonate of soda through the bottom rack and run a rinse cycle to refresh the smell. For extra-clean dishes pop half a lemon onto the top shelf during the wash cycle.

KITCHEN STORAGE & ORGANISATION

If you want to feel comfortable and enjoy cooking in the kitchen, it is important to be sure it is well laid out. This does not have to mean getting in the professional kitchen fitters and spending lots of money. Most people now buy ready-made kitchens or the house comes with the kitchen included. Unfortunately just because an 'expert' designed it, this does not mean that you will have all the right appliances and necessary work-surfaces. Nor does it mean that things will have been set out sensibly – all too often things are put where they look nice, or where they will fit most conveniently.

Often, when you have worked in the

kitchen for a while you will want to change things around. While you may not be able to rearrange the cupboards or big appliances, you can usually rearrange how you store and use things. Think carefully before you fill shelves and cupboards and work backwards: put the most important things in the most accessible places, such as the front of a low shelf, then less important things behind or above. Utensils such as large pots and pans and party-size serving plates can go on top shelves or at the back of a deep base cupboard.

If you are a busy cook you might like to keep everyday equipment close at hand and leave the mixer or food processor out on the work surface. This way, you can reach them easily and avoid wasting time and effort taking them out and putting them away each time. Put the smaller whisks, spoons, peelers and slicers into a jar or utensil holder on the back of the work surface or in a corner where space is not otherwise used so that they are at hand and easy to see. Because such things are different shapes and sizes, drawers are easily cluttered with these items. If space is really tight – say in a small galley kitchen or an apartment where the living room and kitchen are open plan – consider fitting wall-mounted shelves and a magnetic knife rack. Small shelves can take a surprising amount of small spice or herb jars along with the coffee canister and tea caddy.

STORAGE AIDS
Protect your Tupperware from stains by spraying with non-stick cooking oil before pouring in tomato-based sauces; but remember too that portions of lasagne, stew or soups freeze just as well in empty butter spread cartons as in fancy, branded containers.

To open stubborn lids on jars, tap with the back of a knife in an anti-clockwise direction five or six times. Loosening under the lid with a knife also helps to break the airseal and makes jars easier to pop open. Or try getting a firmer grip on a tight-fitting lid by winding a thick elastic band around it. Jars can be recycled too (see Glassware, p52). Small glass yoghurt jars with plastic lids are particularly useful, as the lids are easy to wash and won't rust.

Save your shop-bought bread bags and ties, which make perfect storage bags for your own home-made bread. If you find your roll of clingfilm hard to handle, store it in the fridge or freezer and it will roll out for you without sticking. When wrapping food in tin foil, remember to wrap tightly for storing but loosely for cooking.

Shop Wisely

1. If you're shopping for a large household, organise a major shop for non-perishables goods – weekly, fortnightly or monthly depending on the cash, transport and storage space available. Top up with forays for fresh fruit and vegetables, bread and fish.

2. Never go grocery shopping on an empty stomach: you will buy all the goodies you do not need and probably forget about the essentials you do need. Before you leave the house, go through the kitchen cupboards and make a list of exactly what you need. Shops are designed to tempt you into buying what you do not need. Stick to your list – though maybe not religiously!

3. If you don't have the use of a car it may make sense to shop locally, rather than add the hassle and expense of bus or taxi journeys. But consider doing an occasional big supermarket shop to stock up supplies. Maybe arrange to go with a friend and share the taxi cost.

4. Sometimes life gets in the way of shopping. We might feel too sniffly to brave the weather, or something urgent comes up. It is good to know you can put together a square meal from the store cupboard – but likewise with a special meal. If unexpected visitors turn up, you may need to provide food at short notice or add to what you have already prepared without going to the shops.

5. Stock up on foods that will form the basis of a meal in an emergency or that can be used to stretch a meal: pasta, tinned tomatoes, tinned tuna and rice are all useful. Keep some emergency standby foods in the freezer: ready-made pastry and pitta bread for example, or fish fingers, peas and oven chips.

Real Bargains

When you are out shopping it is all too easy to fall for a bargain only to realise later that it may have been a complete waste of money. When buying meat, you may save by choosing a fatty cut rather than a leaner, more tender piece of meat, but you have to then take into consideration the time and energy/fuel it will take to cook. It may be a bargain if the family actually like the cut you have bought, but if you have to cut off the fat and simply throw it away then you may find that, weight for weight, you have saved nothing. In the same way it is only worth buying 'own brand' items in supermarkets if the people eating them actually like them.

If you live near a big supermarket you can sometimes get good bargains just before closing time or late on Saturday afternoon. Prices are often slashed on fresh dairy foods like cream, and on chilled items with short sell-by dates. Good value can be on offer in the vegetable and fruit section but don't get carried away: six punnets of kiwi fruits at 20 cent each are no bargain if they go off before you can use them up. Think before you buy, and be sure you have time to make jam from those bargain plums, banana bread with those very ripe bananas or soup from all those mushrooms.

Reduce Waste

Good storage habits will keep your food in top condition for longer and stave off unnecessary wastage, which is good news for your nutrition, for your budget and for the world in which we live, where the growing challenges of global food security and shortages make the avoidance of food wastage more important than ever.

FRUIT & VEG: If you tend to buy all your vegetables at once, pop them into a large plastic bag, cut a few holes in it for ventilation and add a piece of coal. Hang on the clothes line and the vegetables will remain fresh.

When storing potatoes or other vegetables, keep them away from onions which make things break down more easily. Always store potatoes away from sunlight – inside a bucket of garden soil is ideal, but inside a cool, dark cupboard is good too. Put a few apples into the paper bag with potatoes to stop them sprouting. Root vegetables can be stored hung up in a string bag. Or wrap carrots and parsnips in newspaper and store in a dark place.

Lettuce leaves will stay fresh longer if washed in water to which a little vinegar has been added. Dry well and store in the bottom drawer of the fridge. To extend its shelf life, wrap celery in tin foil before refrigerating. Broccoli will stay greener if kept in a paper bag in the fridge, while your fresh tomatoes will last longer if stored stem-side down. Pull your bananas apart when you get home from the store to keep them fresh for longer, or leave them connected at the stem to ripen faster. Unripe avocados will ripen faster in a brown paper bag, and especially if you leave them in a warm place such as the hotpress.

MEAT & DAIRY: Storing meat correctly is simple enough but important to get right. Always keep raw meat on a lower shelf so that it cannot drip down onto other foods and contaminate them. Never wash a raw bird before cooking as you will simply spread rather than eliminate any bacteria present (and the heat of cooking will kill these off anyway).

Cheese should be kept in a specified cheese dish rather than in the fridge. A sugar cube placed in the cheese dish prevents mould. If you don't have a cheese dish, wrap cheese in a piece of muslin moistened with vinegar and it will keep fresh. Moisten the cloth again as it dries out.

To keep milk or cream from souring in hot weather, stir in a small quantity of bicarbonate of soda. However, if it's sour milk you're after, add a teaspoonful of vinegar or lemon to one cup of milk. If cream will not whip properly, add the white of an egg and chill before whipping it up again. Cream will keep longer if you add a splash of brandy.

OTHER BITS & BOBS: To keep bread from going mouldy quickly, regularly wash out your bread bin, dry thoroughly and wipe down with vinegar. Stock cubes stored in the fridge will crumble much better, while fridge-chilled salt will keep dry and flow freely.

Pop a few sugar cubes into your biscuit tin to keep the biscuits crisp and fresh. An apple placed in the cake tin will help keep the cake moist. A large cake will keep moist longer if you add a teaspoon of glycerine to the mixture before cooking. Or a couple of tablespoons of marmalade added to a fruit cake mixture works in a similar fashion and will add a delicious flavour to boot – plus it's a good way of using up runny marmalade.

If home-made marmalade has become very runny, reset it by boiling with Jif lemon juice, allowing about seven or eight tablespoons to every 2kg (4lb) of fruit originally used. To rescue honey that has gone hard, simply stand the jar in a bowl of warm water to restore its natural texture.

Love Your Leftovers

1. Refresh tired bread rolls and day-old baguettes in minutes. Preheat the oven to its highest temperature, run the bread under the cold tap for a second and pop in the oven for three minutes.

2. Crumb stale bread by popping in the oven to fully dry out, and blitzing in the blender. Consider flavouring it with some chopped herbs before storing in an airtight container in the freezer.

3. Grate bits of stale cheese and store in an airtight container in the freezer. This will keep for three weeks and is useful for fillings and cheese sauce.

4. Revive wilted lettuce, celery and radishes by soaking first in lukewarm water and then in ice cold water to which a glass of vinegar and a teaspoon of sugar has been added. Good for flushing out insects too.

5. Keep a special bag in the freezer for leftover cooked vegetables. When you have enough for soup, thaw and purée in the blender with vegetable, chicken or beef stock. This can be used to thicken soups, stews and sauces.

6. Save the water used to boil vegetables as a home-made stock for soups and gravies, or re-use for cooking pasta or rice. You can freeze it until ready to use – just make sure to label it before putting in the freezer.

7. Old potatoes can blacken once cooked. Adding a squeeze of lemon juice halfway through cooking when boiling helps prevent discolouration.

8. Freeze up ice-cubes of leftover wine and use for stews and casseroles or thaw them out and use to marinate meat. You could add some chopped leftover herbs to flavour the wine too.

9. Mash and freeze very ripe bananas in one-cup portions for later use in baking, or you can peel them and freeze them whole in plastic bags.

10. Soften hardened brown sugar by transferring to a wide bowl, covering with a damp cloth and leaving overnight.

Maintenance & DIY

Many of us remember growing up with schoolbooks which clearly showed mammies in the kitchen and daddies in the garden. Now we know that life doesn't have to be so clear cut – and rarely is – and that changing plugs and hammering nails are all as very doable as baking cakes and searing steaks. Of course we're not born knowing how to do all these things, but rather learn by paying attention when someone else is doing them. If you found yourself zoning out around DIY matters rather than clueing in, it's not too late to change your ways. It's all about finding ways to remember the little details, such as which wire to place where when changing a plug: Blue (BL) to the left (L); Brown (BR) to the right (R).

Much of it is common sense but useful tips can be learnt from others' experiences, such as the person who learnt to hold a nail with a clothes peg when hammering it in (hence preventing bashing your fingers – ouch!). To drill a hole in the ceiling, drilling through an old plastic bottle will prevent the dust from getting in your eyes. If you are drilling holes in mirrors, tiles or plaster, covering the mark with masking tape first will prevent the surface from cracking. You can remove the tape afterwards.

How to...
Maintain a Smooth-running House

1. A wobbly table can be stabilised by glueing a little something to the base of the problematic leg: a piece of wine cork measured carefully will do the job nicely.

2. Petroleum jelly will loosen stiff latches and bolts, and vegetable oil can be sprayed into sticky locks.

3. Squeaky floorboards can be quietened by sprinkling talcum powder between them or dusting with French chalk.

4. Squeaky hinges can be sprayed with a light cooking oil. Rubbing hinges with a cucumber also works well.

5. If a drawer is sticking, remove it fully and run a wax candle on its runners.

6. Hush a creaking door by rubbing all the joints in the hinges with a lead pencil and swinging the door back and forth a few times to work the lead in. You may need to repeat but it should do the trick.

7. If an electric plug is repeatedly proving difficult to pull out, rub its prongs with a soft lead pencil before plugging back in.

8. For a door that is sticking, rub some chalk down the edge where it meets the frame and close it over: the chalk will leave a mark on the frame showing where the door is sticking, and this can then be sanded or planed down as needed.

9. Save money on heating bills in older houses by blocking up old unused chimneys with plastic foam, old pillows or worn-out clothes.

10. If you don't have double glazing, insulate draughty windows with a layer of insulating window film on the glass. Alternatively, consider lining the curtains (see p29).

Painting & Decorating

Doing your own painting and decorating can be very satisfying and has extra benefits too: painting in particular makes for a great work-out for upper arm muscles (goodbye bingo wings!) and is a great way of burning off extra calories. If you find the smell of paint overpowering, adding a tablespoon of vanilla essence to the tin of paint will help to neutralise the smell. To look after your hands, opt for baby oil, shaving foam or shampoo to soften and remove paint rather than white spirits, which can be quite drying.

You'll need to prepare surfaces before painting. Sugar soap is ideal for stripping a build-up of dirt and grime off walls and ceilings.

Getting started can be the biggest challenge, and choosing the right colours and tones in particular. Always bring home testers of paint and try each out in a corner of the room before committing to any one – you may have to live with it for some time to come. Once you've finished painting a room, hold on to the spare paint for touching up scuffs and scratches. If there's not much left, pour it into a jar and label it so you know which room you have used it on. If you have a leftover tin of paint that you are not ready to use, store it upside down (with the lid very secure of course!). This way the skin that occurs under the lid will be in the bottom when turned back the right way up.

Once you've finished a painting job, take the time to store everything away properly and to finish up the edges nicely. You can remove hardened paint spots quickly and easily from windows with nail-varnish remover, or scrape small spots gently with a razor blade (just take care not to scratch the glass). Soak used paint brushes in hot vinegar and wash well in warm soapy water.

For little jobs like touching up flooring with varnish or staining or painting a limited area, an easy way to avoid cleaning a dirty paint brush is simply not to use one. Instead, use a piece of sponge held in between a clothes peg, both of which you can discard afterwards.

A Basic Tool Kit

A good cook never blames their tools. They don't have to, because they know the value in investing in good ones. Likewise, for developing your handy skills about the house, having the right tools is the best start to doing a good job. Handy tools worth investing in include:

• A cordless drill or screwdriver set – you'll need to be able to tackle both flathead and Phillips screws.
• A pair of pliers, or two, and maybe an adjustable wrench – for gripping things of various sizes.
• A hammer and nails – go for a weight that you're comfortable holding, and opt for a claw hammer which can pull out old nails as well as knocking in new ones.
• Measuring tape and spirit level – to check the dimensions before hammering or drilling.
• Chalk – to mark where the nails will go once you've measured.

Chapter 4

Like Mam Used to Make

PANCAKE TUESDAY • MOTHER'S DAY • ST PATRICK'S DAY
MIDSUMMER • SUMMER PICNIC • HALLOWEEN
THE LATE LATE TOY SHOW • CHRISTMAS • NOLLAIG NA MBAN
THE BIRTHDAY PARTY

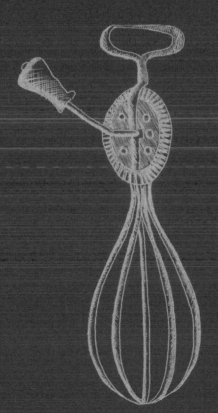

Like Mam Used to Make

Family meals are as much about the occasion as they are about what's on the table. There's something about the ritual of annual seasonal meals that makes them even more special every year they are served: the perennial birthday cake particular to your family; the pile of pancakes that marks the beginning of Lent and countdown to Easter; the Christmas cake cooked up well in advance and stored in the same old biscuit tin as always. These are the dishes we hope will taste just as we remember them always tasting: just like mam used to make. They are special because we return to them year after year, a little older, a little wiser, but still together as a family. Even if some members are missing, returning to these dishes returns those missing loved ones to us.

Pancake Tuesday

Who doesn't love Pancake Tuesday? It's a national institution in Ireland, coming around every Shrove Tuesday as a little treat before the beginning of Lent on Ash Wednesday. Of course it's worth mastering a good pancake recipe for use throughout the year too. If pancakes are that much fun to make, why not make them a regular breakfast treat? Your children will thank you for it, and it's a good way to sneak some healthy fruit toppings into their regular diet.

Back in the Day...

"My mother's pancakes consisted of flour, salt, egg, milk and dripping for frying, cooked in a pan on the heart of the old turf fire. They would be served with ice-cream and were a delicious treat for us."
Mary O'Reilly, Mayo

Buttermilk Pancakes

Anne O'Connor, Wexford

The addition of buttermilk to these pancakes combines with the bicarbonate of soda to make lovely fluffy pancakes. They don't need extra lemon juice as they are acidic enough; better to opt for a sweet or savoury accompaniment.

Makes 6 pancakes

INGREDIENTS
- 225g (8oz) plain flour
- 1 level teaspoon bicarbonate of soda
- 1 teaspoon salt
- 1 teaspoon caster sugar
- 1 egg
- 400ml (¾ pint) buttermilk
- 100g butter

to serve
- maple syrup, honey, home-made jam or crisp grilled rashers

what you'll need
- small frying pan or pancake pan, about 23cm (9in)

ICA Tip
Unlike other pancake batters which benefit from standing before use, this mixture must be used immediately. Using the smallest pan you have will help them rise well.

1. Sieve together the flour, soda and salt into a large mixing bowl, add the sugar and mix well.

2. In a separate bowl, whisk the egg into the buttermilk. Slowly add the liquid to the dry ingredients, beating well until you have a smooth batter the consistency of a gooey paste.

3. Heat a small non-stick frying pan over a medium heat, melt a knob of butter on it and add a ladleful of batter. Cook for three or four minutes or until the mixture rises and bubbles on top before flipping and cooking on the other side for two or three minutes.

4. Serve immediately as you cook the remainder, adding a little knob of butter or slick of oil for each new pancake. Alternatively transfer to a warm oven where you can stack them until ready to serve.

Healthy Pancake Fillings

BRID FITZPATRICK, KILKENNY

Pancakes are a great base for many flavours: here are three easy fruit fillings to add to your repertoire.

for the banana and lemon filling
- 4 bananas, sliced
- 3 tablespoons Golden Syrup
- 1–2 tablespoons fresh lemon juice
- 1 small tub fromage frais

Combine the banana, syrup and juice in a small saucepan and simmer gently for one minute. Spoon into warm pancakes and serve with fromage frais.

for the apple and blackberry filling
- 450g (1lb) cooking apples
- 225g (8oz) blackberries
- 2 tablespoons brown sugar
- 3 tablespoons water

Peel apples and slice into pan with blackberries, add sugar and water and cook gently for about 10 minutes until fruit is soft. Spoon into warm pancakes and serve.

for the orange and blueberry filling
- 4 medium oranges
- 2 cups blueberries
- 1 small tub natural yoghurt

Peel and segment oranges, combine with the blueberries in a small saucepan and heat gently to warm through. Spoon into warm pancakes and serve with natural yoghurt.

ICA Tip
If you use a meat baster to 'squeeze' your pancake batter onto the hot griddle you can have perfectly shaped pancakes every time!

Handle Eggs

1. Eggs should generally be stored at room temperature and not in the fridge, especially when making a sponge cake. Correct storage also helps prevent the shells from cracking when they are boiled.

2. Store eggs in their original cartons to keep track of the best before date. Eggs will keep fresh for longer if stored with the pointed end uppermost.

3. If in doubt about an egg's freshness, immerse in a bowl of cold water. The air pocket in an egg expands as it matures. Therefore, if the egg sinks to the bottom of the water, it is fresh, but if it floats to the surface, it is stale and should be discarded.

4. Egg yolks will keep in the refrigerator for several days if covered with a little cold water. When separating a yolk from its white, try to keep the yolk intact so you can remember how many yolks are there. This is easiest done by cracking the egg into a clean hand and allowing the white to run through the fingers into a bowl.

5. Egg yolks are useful for making fresh mayonnaise and aioli, which can be flavoured with garlic or herbs. Simply whisk two seasoned egg yolks with a tablespoon of Dijon mustard and very slowly drizzle in 275ml (½ pint) of oil while still whisking. Once the yolks and oil begin to emulsify, you can add the oil in faster, and finish with a little vinegar or lemon juice to taste.

6. Egg whites will keep for up to two weeks stored in an airtight container in the fridge. They also freeze well. If you have mixed the whites of several eggs, remember that 30g (1oz) of egg white is equivalent to the white of one average egg.

7. Egg whites are useful for meringues and for glazing cakes. When putting almond icing on Christmas cakes, an initial coating of egg white will help it adhere to the cake.

8. If you run short of eggs when making a fruit cake, mix ½ teaspoon bicarbonate of soda with a dessertspoon of vinegar and add to the batter after all the other ingredients to substitute for two eggs. This trick was commonly used by Irish housewives at Christmas time when there was a shortage of eggs.

Mother's Day

Mother's Day might seem to many to be a heavily commercialised concept designed to sell over-priced schmaltzy cards and bunches of flowers, but you could also use it as inspiration to make something personal for your mother, your mother-in-law or even for the mother of your grandchildren. For many of us, nothing transports us to our childhood like the taste of creamy country butter on fresh home-made soda bread. What better way to honour our generations of mothers than with these simple, wholesome flavours and the memories they evoke?

You can pick up some very good brands of country butter today, or you could try making your own. Commercial butter will have a longer shelf life but you can't beat the freshness of home-made butter. If you do make your own butter, you have the added benefit of fresh buttermilk to be used in the kitchen or around the house.

Back in the Day...

"My mother used to make lovely bread in the cake tin over the oven fire. She would put on a really good coal fire, let the tin redden up and the lid of the cake tin would be heated on it and placed on the top. This procedure would continue until the bread was cooked."
Sarah Buckley, Wexford

Breda's Family White Soda Bread

Breda McDonald, Kilkenny

Although you could use buttermilk for this recipe, the use of sour cream is wonderful for added richness and a developed flavour.

Makes one 900g (2lb) loaf

INGREDIENTS
- 450g (1lb) plain flour
- 1 teaspoon bicarbonate of soda
- 1 teaspoon baking powder
- 1 dessertspoon caster sugar
- pinch of salt
- 50g (2oz) butter
- 1 egg
- 275ml (½ pint) sour cream
- extra flour for dusting

to serve
- lashings of country butter

what you'll need
- baking tray

1. Preheat the oven to 170°C/325°F/Gas 3. Grease a flat baking tray and dust with a little flour.

2. Sieve the flour, bicarbonate of soda and baking powder into a large mixing bowl. Add the sugar and salt and mix well. Add the butter and rub it in using the tips of your fingers to create a fine breadcrumb consistency.

3. In a small bowl whisk together the sour cream and the egg with a fork, to combine fully. Pour the liquid into the dry ingredients and mix until a soft sticky dough has been achieved.

4. Transfer onto a lightly floured work surface and knead gently. Shape into a large round or rectangle, transfer onto the prepared baking tray and flatten with your hands. Dip a sharp knife in some flour, cut a cross on the bread and dust generously with extra flour.

5. Bake in preheated oven for 40–45 minutes until golden brown. Allow to cool on a wire tray and serve with lashings of country butter.

Make Country Butter

1. If it's your first time making country butter, you could use your kitchen mixer, carefully. Plastic churns are available here in Ireland, or you could invest in a glass churning jar (available online), which produces the best butter.

2. Traditionally, country butter was made from the cream that rose to the top of raw, un-homogenised milk but you can use shop-bought cream: depending on the fat content, 1 litre (1¾ pints) will give about 450g (1lb) of butter, and 500ml (1 pint) of buttermilk.

3. Sterilise your equipment carefully. Scald a heatproof churn or mixer with boiling water, rinse with cold water and dry thoroughly. A glass churner should be washed with lukewarm salty water.

4. Chill the cream to about 7°C (45°F) before churning: the cold temperature slows down the churning but helps the buttermilk to separate from the solids, thereby increasing its shelf life.

5. Fill the churn about one third full. If using a mixer, cover the bowl with a cloth or foil to prevent splashing.

6. Churn or beat slowly and gently for about 10–15 minutes or until the butter solids separate from the buttermilk to form wheat grain shapes. If using a mixer, take care not to over whip the buttermilk back into the butter, which will cause it to spoil within a few days.

7. Strain off the buttermilk and reserve for making brown bread and pancakes (see p71), or for feeding chickens (see p122).

8. Wash the butter inside the churn or mixer bowl until the water is clear: ideally, you'll change the water three times before a final immersion in salted water (about three tablespoons of table salt to five litres of water). Leave to stand for an hour or so before straining.

9. You will be left with small grains of butter. These can be used directly in baking, or shaped into blocks of butter. You may want to squeeze the grains with the back of a spoon to release any trapped buttermilk.

10. If making a small amount of butter, you can shape it on a square wooden board with butter paddles or Scotch hands. Steep both in boiling water first, scrub with salt and leave for a few minutes. Shape the butter as desired, wrap in greaseproof paper and store in the fridge.

St Patrick's Day

Today, St Patrick's Day is celebrated by the Irish diaspora all around the world, and we see many great cities hosting sophisticated parades. Broad rivers, landmark sky-scrapers and ancient monuments all turn green for the day. But it is in the small towns and villages around Ireland that the spirit of St Patrick's Day really lives on, when local communities come together to play music and don the shamrock just as they have been doing for so many years. If you're looking for the perfect party food for 17th March, you can't go wrong with baked ham and colcannon, followed by a perfect Irish coffee.

Back in the Day...

"Every St Patrick's Day we would get up early to go pick the shamrock in the front field. We proudly wore it to mass and for the remainder of the day. We lived on a farm and were self-sufficient, having lots of chickens, ducks, geese and turkeys. We also had vegetables of every kind to choose from. That day, after a lunch of our own lovely fresh food, we headed for Castlebar to take part in the St Patrick's Day parade."

Mary O'Reilly, Mayo

ICA Tip
The addition of the vinegar is optional but will help to draw out the salty taste of the ham and improve its flavour.

Baked Ham

CASTLETOWN GUILD MEMBERS, LAOIS

*Every Irish household used to eat boiled bacon and cabbage as part of their everyday diet,
but when it was time to celebrate, that bacon would be glazed and baked in the oven.
The resulting ham can be served hot or cold, making it ideal party food
if people are coming and going.*

Serves 8

INGREDIENTS

- 1 ham fillet, about 2kg (4lb)
- 1 carrot, peeled and roughly chopped
- 1 celery stick, roughly chopped
- 1 onion, peeled and quartered
- 60ml (4 tablespoons) cider or white wine vinegar (optional)
- ½ teaspoon grated nutmeg
- 4 bay leaves

for the glaze

- 2 heaped tablespoons Demerara sugar
- 1 heaped tablespoon mustard
- milk, enough to bind
- 15–20 cloves

to serve

- colcannon or boiled cabbage, see p82

1. Soak the ham in cold water for a couple of hours or overnight. Drain well, combine with the vegetables in a large pot and cover with fresh cold water. Add the vinegar, nutmeg and bay leaves and bring to the boil. Reduce to a simmer and cook for about 90 minutes, or 20 minutes per lb.

2. Remove from the heat and set aside to cool in the cooking liquor. Once cool enough to handle, remove ham from the liquid and trim the rind and some of the excess fat, leaving about 1cm (½ inch) layer of fat. Meanwhile, preheat the oven to 170°C/325°F/Gas 3.

3. Transfer the trimmed ham to a baking tray. Score the fat with a sharp knife to make criss-cross incisions and stud the corners of each diamond with cloves. Blend the sugar and mustard with enough milk to form a paste, and cover the fat with this glaze.

4. Brown the glazed ham in a pre-heated oven for 30–40 minutes. Remove from the oven and allow to rest for five minutes before slicing.

Colcannon

ADA VANCE, CAVAN

Colcannon is a popular variation on mashed potatoes and cabbage. It is traditionally served at Halloween time (with lucky charms and foil-wrapped coins hidden through it) but works well in mid-March when the winter crop of kale will be available.

Serves 6

INGREDIENTS

- 6 large floury potatoes, such as Roosters, peeled and halved
- 225g (8oz) curly kale cabbage (or Savoy cabbage)
- 85g (3oz) butter, or three generous knobs
- 3 tablespoons milk
- 6 scallions (spring onions), finely chopped
- salt and pepper

to garnish
- 1–2 tablespoons finely chopped parsley

ICA Tip
A teaspoon of sugar added to boiling potatoes improves the flavour and makes them more floury.

1. Boil the potatoes in salted water until tender, about 15–20 minutes. Mash well and set aside.

2. Wash the kale thoroughly, removing the thicker stalks, and finely slice the tender leaves. In a lidded, heavy-based pan, melt a knob of butter with a little water and a pinch of salt. Add the kale, cover and cook gently until tender, about 15 minutes. Add another knob of butter and set aside.

3. Combine the milk and scallions in a large pan and bring to the boil. Fold in the kale and mashed potatoes. Beat well until fluffy, season and serve with the chopped parsley and an extra knob of butter.

How to...

Make an Irish Coffee

1. Choosing the right glassware is important. You want a glass that is thick enough both to withstand the heat and to preserve it. There's nothing more disappointing than going to all the trouble involved and then serving up a lukewarm drink.

2. A wine glass is the traditional shape, or a glass mug of the kind used for lattes and hot chocolate is a good option, as the handle makes it easy for the drinker to hold. Alternatively, wrap a folded napkin around the glass before serving.

3. Preheat the glass by scalding with freshly boiled water. To be on the safe side, a teaspoon inserted in the glass first will help conduct some of the heat and prevent more delicate wine glasses from cracking.

4. Be sure to use the best freshly brewed coffee you can – a rich and robust blend will stand up well to the whiskey.

5. The cream should be whipped until it just begins to hold a figure of eight but so that it can still pour. Over-whipping the cream will encourage it to sink.

6. A teaspoon or two of sugar is crucial in helping the cream to float. You can serve an unsweetened Irish coffee but it is unlikely to hold its cream head for long.

7. Add the coffee first and then stir in the sugar until fully dissolved. Add the shot of Irish whiskey last, so as not to cool the glass down first.

8. Be sure to dissolve the sugar fully in the base of the glass before adding the cream: caster sugar will dissolve quicker than brown sugar.

9. To add the cream, heat two spoons in the hot coffee and use one to gently ladle the cream over the back of the other and onto the surface of the coffee.

10. Sprinkle with a couple of roasted coffee beans and serve piping hot.

Midsummer Days
& Nights

"Dry March, wet May, plenty of corn, plenty of hay. Wet March, dry May, little corn, little hay." Horseleap Streamstown Guild Members, Westmeath

There's a lot to celebrate in midsummer, whether it's a successful bout of haymaking or the long stretch in the evenings. In some parts of Ireland (and particularly the west coast where the evening stretch is the longest), the tradition of the summertime bonfire night lives on strong. Falling close to the summer solstice, the weeks building up to the big night are spent gathering turf, timber and anything else that can be found for the fire. Music is often provided by local musicians to ensure lots of singing and dancing around the bonfire late into the night.

Back in the Day…

"I have always enjoyed the annual midsummer bonfire night, both growing up in Leitrim and now in Sligo where I live today. It is celebrated every year on 23rd June, when the communities of rural towns and villages light fires and gather around to enjoy some music and food which they bring along. It is a great get-together for family and local community. For about a week before the night, the teenagers go around to the local houses gathering up materials for the fire. The younger children come along with their parents who are always there to supervise the fire on the night itself.

Known to some as St John's Eve, the ancient custom dates back to pagan times, with its roots in pre-Christian Irish society when the Celts honoured the goddess Aine, who is the Celtic equivalent of Venus and Aphrodite. In some rural areas, it is the tradition to take the ashes from the fire and spread them over the land as a blessing for the protection of crops.

It was only in recent years, while chatting with some ICA friends from different parts of Ireland, that I discovered that this custom is not a nationwide practice – the ladies from the midlands and the south of the country weren't familiar with the annual bonfire. I hope it is a practice that will continue to be enjoyed into the future."
Mary Harkin, Sligo

Haymaker's Beef

Mary Harkin, Sligo

An old recipe for a rich tasty stew which was a favourite with haymakers.
You can easily double the quantities and freeze the extra servings
– or reheat and eat the next day when it will be even tastier!

Serves 4

INGREDIENTS
- 1kg (2lb) stewing beef, cubed
- 1 onion, sliced
- 80ml (3fl oz) wine or cider vinegar
- 50g (2oz) soft dark brown sugar
- 5 whole peppercorns
- 1 bouquet garni
- pinch of ground cloves
- pinch of ground mace
- pinch of salt
- 570ml (1 pint) beer
- 275ml (½ pint) water or beef or vegetable stock

ICA Tip
Marinating any red meat in vinegar helps to break down the fibres, as does slow cooking, making for extra tender meat in the final dish.

1. Place the meat and onion in a large mixing bowl. In a separate bowl or jug, combine all the remaining ingredients except the beer and pour over the beef. Cover and leave to stand overnight, turning the meat occasionally so that it is evenly marinated.

2. The next day, tip the contents of the bowl into a large pot and pour in the beer. Add 275ml (½ pint) water or stock. Bring to the boil before reducing the heat, covering and simmering for two or three hours or until the beef is tender. You may need to top up with extra stock or water if needed.

3. Remove the bouquet garni and serve with lots of floury potatoes or home-made bread for soakage.

Lemon Barley Water

Lily Champ, Laois

This is a very refreshing drink on a hot sunny day, served with ice or straight from the fridge. This recipe can be easily doubled or tripled to make larger quantities, but remember that you'll be diluting it down before serving.

Makes about 850ml
(1½ pints)

INGREDIENTS
- 50g (2oz) pearl barley
- 1 lemon (organic if possible), peeled and pared
- 110g (4oz) granulated sugar
- 100ml (3.5fl oz) lemon juice (about three lemons)

ICA Tips
You will get more juice from lemons, limes and oranges if they are warmed through before squeezing. Try blasting in the microwave for about 15 seconds on high, or pop into a hot oven for a few minutes. Roll the lemon under your palm before halving and squeezing.

1. Rinse the pearl barley well in cold water. Drain, transfer to a saucepan and cover with cold water. Bring to the boil and allow to boil for three minutes before draining.

2. Return the barley to the rinsed-out saucepan, add the thinly pared lemon peel and one litre of cold water and return to the boil. Cover and simmer for 20 minutes.

3. Tip the contents of the saucepan into a sieve placed over a large bowl to capture the liquid. The cooked barley can be kept for use in a stew.

4. Stir the sugar into the hot barley water and leave until cold. Add lemon juice and store in a clean bottle in the fridge. When needed, dilute to taste with tap water or sparkling water if preferred.

Summer Picnic

Summer comes – and goes – pretty swiftly here in Ireland, sometimes several times in one day! The important thing is to be ready to make the most of it when it does arrive, and for as long as it lasts. Picnics and barbecues must be impromptu affairs, and having a few standby picnic ideas up your sleeve means you needn't be caught out. These two recipes use ingredients you could easily have on hand: smoked mackerel and cream cheese from the fridge, scallions and celery from the salad drawer, flour from the pantry and cooking apples from the garden.

Smoked Mackerel Pâté

Susan Ryan, Kildare

*This simple recipe makes a great standby for an impromptu summer picnic.
You can use peppered smoked mackerel for extra seasoning and
low fat cream cheese for a healthier option.*

Serves 4 as part of a picnic

INGREDIENTS
- 300g (10oz) smoked mackerel
- 85g (3oz) cream cheese with chives
- 2 scallions (spring onion), finely sliced
- 1 stick of celery, finely chopped
- ½ lemon, juice only
- salt and pepper

to serve
- crackers or oatcakes

1. Remove mackerel flesh from its skin, avoiding the bones which run along the centre, and flake into a bowl.

2. Add the cream cheese, scallions and celery, mix well to bind, and mix in the lemon juice to taste.

3. Check seasoning and chill until ready to use.

ICA Tips
This will keep well for several days as the smoked fish and cream cheese both have a generous shelf life.

Kerry Apple Cake

MARY O'REILLY, MAYO

This traditional cake resembles sweetened white soda bread. It's an easy one to throw together in the time it takes to get the kids ready to hit the beach on a sunny morning, and it's ideal for one-handed eating at the end of a picnic.

Serves 8

INGREDIENTS
- 225g (8oz) plain flour
- 1 teaspoon bicarbonate of soda
- pinch of salt
- 85g (3oz) margarine
- 85g (3oz) sugar
- 3 cooking apples
- 150ml (¼ pint) milk
- 1 egg, beaten
- 1–2 drops of vanilla extract (or lemon essence)
- cold water, about 1–2 tablespoons

what you'll need
- 20cm (8in) round cake tin

ICA Tip
Don't pre-slice the apples or they will oxidate and brown. There is such a thing as being too organised!

1. Preheat the oven to 180°C/350°F/Gas 4. Grease a round cake tin.

2. Sieve the flour, bicarbonate of soda and salt together into a large mixing bowl. Add the margarine and rub in to resemble fine breadcrumbs. Add the sugar.

3. Peel and thinly slice the apples, and add together with the milk. Add the beaten egg, vanilla extract and enough cold water to make a stiff batter.

4. Put into a greased tin and bake in preheated oven for about 45 minutes or until an inserted skewer comes out clean. This can be served hot with custard or allowed to cool fully and used as a moist cake – perfect for picnics!

Pack a Picnic

1. Impromptu picnics can be easily catered for with a little imagination and a few store cupboard basics: a tin or two of tuna or salmon, sweetcorn, mayonnaise and a little lemon can go a long way, as can smoked fish, tinned sardines and pre-sliced ham. Cheese and fruit will stretch it out, while vacuum-packed tortillas are a good store-cupboard substitute for fresh bread. Don't forget to pack some salt and pepper, paper napkins, a sharp knife and a couple of forks.

2. Some dishes are best made at the last minute. Soggy sandwiches can be side-stepped by making up sandwiches as needed, or by storing wet ingredients such as sliced tomatoes separately and adding them before eating. Pack your salad leaves and dressing separately to avoid soggy lettuce. Boiled potatoes for a salad will absorb less oil and taste better if you sprinkle them with a little white wine while still warm. Add the dressing once they have absorbed the wine.

3. When hard-boiling eggs, pierce them with a small sewing needle before adding to the hot salted water to prevent eggshells from cracking and to help remove the shells easily. Boil for eight to ten minutes and rinse under cold water until cooled to prevent the outer yolks from blackening. Tap a ring around the middle of the shell and twist to pull off the two shell halves. Slice with a sharp knife dipped in boiling water to prevent crumbling, and wrap each egg individually in clingfilm for easy storage.

4. Picnic baskets and coolers are handy if you're likely to get a lot of use out of them, but you can improvise with recycled bits and pieces. Plastic trays from pre-packed foods make excellent disposable plates for family parties and picnics, while lidded takeaway containers are good for sandwich fillers and salads.

5. Pick up some zip-up freezer bags from your local supermarket, and use to keep drinks and chilled foods cool. Pop a couple of ice-packs into the freezer the night before or make your own by placing a wet sponge in a zip-lock bag and freezing. Alternatively, freeze a three-quarters full bottle of water to double up as an ice-pack and drinking water once it melts.

Halloween

It was the Irish who brought Halloween as we know it to the rest of the world. Here in Ireland it has its roots in the Celtic Samhain festival, a time when ceremonial fires would be lit and the souls of the dead were thought to walk the earth for one night, with loved ones returning to their homes, but more mischievous spirits roaming the roads too. It was also the time of autumnal bounty, when crops would be gathered and cattle slaughtered.

Many of the old traditions live on strong on these shores: the lighting of neighbourhood bonfires, dressing up and visiting the neighbours 'trick or treating', hiding lucky charms in barn brack and colcannon, bobbing for apples and various other seasonal games (see p108 for children's games). Don't forget to stock up on monkey nuts and penny sweets for the visiting children. You might even like to invite them and their parents in and offer them a slice of buttered brack and a perfect cuppa (see p172).

Any self-respecting brack should contain at least a few foil-wrapped coins, but if you want to have fun you could add some other traditional charms. Each should be well-wrapped and each is thought to give its finder a glimpse of their fortune: a thimble for a spinster-to-be, a button for a future bachelor, a scrap of cloth to warn of poverty. As for the ring and coins – they were always the most sought after, being symbols of marriage and wealth.

Back in the Day…

"The Halloween brack was always a real treat with the hidden ring and other surprises. We had to duck for pennies in the basin of water, and try to bite the bobbing apple. We gathered chestnuts and dressed up in our parents' clothes pretending we were adults to scare our neighbours."
Mary O'Reilly, Mayo

Báirín Breac (Barn Brack)

Elizabeth Murphy, Laois

There are many explanations for the exact origins of the name 'barn brack', or Báirín Breac as Gaeilge. The most common is that báirín is an abbreviation of builín aráin, which means loaf of bread, and that breac is the old Gaeilge word for speckled. 'Speckled bread' is a pretty good name for this yeasty, fruity loaf, traditionally spread with country butter and washed down with plenty of tea.

makes 1 large brack

INGREDIENTS
- 350g (12oz) plain flour
- 1 teaspoon salt
- 14g (½oz) dry yeast
- 200ml (7fl oz) mixed milk and water, warmed
- 25g (1oz) sugar
- 25g (1oz) margarine
- 110g (4oz) sultanas
- 25g (1oz) currants
- 25g (1oz) chopped peel
- ¼ teaspoon mixed spice

for the lucky charms
- a small 'gold' ring (from your local thrift store)
- a coin or three

what you'll need
- 1 x 900g (2lb) loaf tin or a deep 18cm (7in) round tin
- greaseproof paper

1. Sieve the flour and salt into a large mixing bowl. Cream the yeast with a teaspoon of the sugar in half of the warm milk and water. Make a well in the centre of the flour, pour in the yeast mixture and sprinkle a little flour on top. Leave for 20 minutes until the yeast activates (it will start to set on the top).

2. Mix in the flour from the edges and the remaining liquid, stirring well with a wooden spoon to combine thoroughly. Using your hand, form into a ball and transfer to a lightly floured surface. Continue to knead for several minutes until the dough is smooth and no longer feels sticky.

3. Wash the mixing bowl, coat it lightly with a little margarine and transfer the smooth dough to it. Cover and set aside somewhere warm (the hotpress is perfect) for about 30 minutes or until it doubles in size. Meanwhile, wrap the lucky charms in greaseproof paper, if using.

4. Transfer the dough back onto a lightly floured surface and press down into a flattened round. Dot with the margarine, scatter over the sugar, fruit, spice and lucky charms and knead well to integrate evenly. Return to the greased bowl for another 30 minutes before transferring to a greased 900g (2lb) loaf tin.

5. Preheat the oven to 180°C/350°F/Gas 4. Set the dough aside until it has risen to the top of the tin, brush with milk and bake for 45–50 minutes, or until an inserted skewer comes out clean.

6. Remove from the oven and allow to cool in the tin for 20 minutes before turning it out onto a wire rack to cool completely.

Use Your Freezer

1. Autumn is a traditional time to think like a squirrel and stockpile food for the leaner winter. It's a good time to stock up the freezer with hearty dishes for the colder days to come.

2. Freezers need to be well-organised in order to be used efficiently and safely. Most important is that foods are rotated regularly, especially in a top-loading deep freezer where it is tempting to simply focus on the recently added items at the surface and forget about what's lurking below.

3. Always label things properly when they're going into the freezer, and be sure to include the date on which you froze the food. Keep some masking tape and a permanent marker handy for home-made labels.

4. It can be helpful to think about how you'd like to use your meat before you freeze it. Beef steaks can be marinated before freezing, and then frozen in individual freezer bags together with excess marinade for a quick and easy supper.

5. Never refreeze thawed out meat, and take extra care with leftovers of food you did not cook yourself, such as takeaways or doggie bags from restaurants.

6. Meat is best thawed slowly – overnight in the fridge is perfect. Wrap it well in several layers of clingfilm. This will help it thaw evenly rather than from the outside in.

7. Frozen fish can be thawed in milk to give the fish a fresher taste. You can use the milk to make the accompanying sauce.

8. Some ingredients are best used straight from the freezer. Frozen peeled ginger can be grated effectively and won't give you that stringy effect you get when grating from fresh. Frozen chocolate can be 'peeled' with a potato peeler to make perfect chocolate shavings.

9. Defrosting chicken fillets or beef steaks to be used in stir-fries can be sliced into strips while still part-frozen: they are easier to slice thinly in this state, and will finish defrosting quicker.

10. Save your leftover stale bread and unwanted heels and blitz in a food processor to make your own bread crumbs. Store these in a re-sealable bag in the freezer, but be sure to make it airtight before freezing.

The Late Late Toy Show

Running on our nation's television sets year in, year out since the 1960s, *The Late Late Show* is an institution in Irish households, but nothing beats the excitement of watching its annual Toy Show. It's really just a great excuse for the little ones to stay up late and pretend they're older than they are, and of course for us big ones to indulge in the festive excitement and pretend we're younger than we are.

The evening is a marathon event, during which important decisions will be made, such as exactly what Santa will be bringing down the chimney. You will want to be well-sustained, so some sweet treats will be welcome. It's also a great excuse to stretch out the excitement of the big night into the previous day, especially if you get the kids involved in baking some snacks for the whole family to enjoy together. Let their creativity run riot by decorating a gingerbread family, with one for everyone in the audience!

You'll want something to dunk those gingery legs and arms into too. To make the perfect cup of cocoa, use the best chocolate you can and be sure to have some thick, whipped cream to dollop on top. For good volume, whip together equal parts of single and double cream, or alternatively beat two egg whites stiffly together with a small carton of double cream. Either way, sweeten to taste with a little caster sugar. Remember that skimmed milk burns easily so, if using, take care to warm gently over a low heat. Rinse the saucepan with cold water first to prevent the milk from burning and sticking to the pot.

Gingerbread Family

Liz Wall, Wicklow

Why make gingerbread men when you can make a gingerbread family? If you don't have cutters, you could draw your own figures on greaseproof paper, cut these out and use as guides to cut around with a sharp knife.

makes about 20

INGREDIENTS
- 350g (12oz) plain flour, plus extra for rolling out
- 2 teaspoons ground ginger
- 1 teaspoon ground cinnamon
- 1 teaspoon bicarbonate of soda
- 125g (4½oz) soft butter
- 175g (6oz) light brown sugar
- 3–4 tablespoons golden syrup
- 1 egg

to decorate
- 140g (5oz) icing sugar
- 1 egg white
- liquid food colouring, about 8–10 drops each
- cake decorations (try mini-Smarties, silver balls, etc)

what you'll need
- plastic piping bags
- 2 baking trays
- greaseproof paper
- gingerbread people cutters (or make your own stencils)

ICA Tip
A well-rinsed eye dropper is an ideal tool to dispense exact quantities of food colouring into food.

1. Sieve the flour, ground spices and bicarbonate of soda into a large mixing bowl or a food processor. Add the butter and rub lightly or blend until the mixture resembles breadcrumbs. Fold in the sugar.

2. Lightly beat the golden syrup and the egg together, add to the crumbed mixture and mix with your hands or pulse in the food processor until it all starts to come together into a loose dough. Transfer to a lightly floured surface and knead gently until smooth. Wrap in clingfim and refrigerate for 20–30 minutes.

3. Preheat the oven to 180°C/350°F/Gas 4. Line two baking trays with greaseproof paper.

4. On a lightly floured surface, roll the dough out to a thickness of about ½cm (¼in). Cut out the gingerbread men and women shapes with cutters.

5. Carefully transfer the gingerbread people onto lined baking trays, being sure to space them out well so that they don't stick to each other when they expand. Re-roll any remaining dough and cut out into more gingerbread people. Bake for 12–15 minutes or until just golden-brown.

6. Meanwhile, to make your own writing icing, in a clean, dry bowl beat an egg white to soft peaks. Gradually sieve in the icing sugar and continue beating to stiff peaks. Divide the icing between several small bowls. Keep one white but add some colouring to the others and stir well until combined. Wrap each with clingfilm and refrigerate until ready to use.

7. Remove the gingerbread from the oven and leave to cool a little on the tray (about 10 minutes) before transferring to a wire rack to cool completely. Transfer the icing into separate plastic piping bags. Cut a small hole in a corner of each bag and pipe the icing over the cooled gingerbread men to decorate. Finish with mini-Smarties or cake decorations of choice.

Christmas

Back in the Day…

"It was always early to bed on Christmas Eve, with the lighted candle glistening in the window, brightening up our darkened bedroom and becoming a welcoming light for weary travellers. Outside, the night is thick with frost and one large star seems to shine brighter in the seasonal galaxy, sending its Christmas cheer like a message from heaven.

The sights and smells of Christmas are all around us. In the corner of the room sits a huge bowl of trifle prepared a few hours earlier by my mother's gentle hands. The bowl is full of a mixture of fruits and sponge soaked in sherry and bound together with strawberry and raspberry jellies. With the aroma wafting over, temptation is strong as I hop out of bed, rush over and dip my fingers into the large bowl to taste the forbidden fruit. A luscious strawberry together with some sherry-soaked sponge becomes my prize. Delicious! Beside the trifle stands a large crock of milk layered with a thick coating of double or even treble cream. As my finger skims over the top, I draw the shape of a star and watch it slowly disappear while I lick my finger and savour the delights of tomorrow's feast.

Suddenly, a noise is heard on the galvanised roof. With one step I'm back in bed, snuggled in under the blankets close to my older sister who is sleeping soundly. I dare not peep out in case I disturb our annual visitor who has travelled so far to fill our stockings with priceless treasures. Maybe I will get the doll with sleeping eyes this year and possibly a pram to wheel her around in. No harm in dreaming as I drift into a happy slumber…"

Patricia Cavanagh, Monaghan

Christmas Cake

MARION LAWLESS, LAOIS

Thanks to all that preserved fruit and alcohol, a home-made Christmas cake should happily keep for six months or more in an airtight tin. It should always be made one month before it is required to allow the flavours to really develop.

Makes a deep 20cm
(8in) cake

INGREDIENTS
- 225g (8oz) light brown sugar
- 170g (6oz) butter or margarine
- 1 orange, juice and zest
- 340g (12oz) sultanas
- 340g (12oz) fruit mix
- 200g (7oz) cherries
- 200ml (7fl oz) whiskey, brandy or poteen
- 110g (4oz) ground almonds
- 110g (4oz) mixed nuts
- 3 large eggs
- 225g (8oz) plain flour
- 1 tablespoon mixed spice

for the topping (optional)
- 2 tablespoons apricot jam
- marzipan (see overpage)
- royal icing (see overpage)
- silver or gold balls, for decoration

what you'll need
- 20cm (8in) round tin
- greaseproof paper

1. Combine the sugar, butter or margarine, orange zest and juice, dried fruit and half of the alcohol in a large saucepan. Slowly bring to the boil, stirring occasionally till the butter has melted. Turn off the heat and leave to cool for 30 minutes.

2. Preheat the oven to 140°C/275°F/Gas 1. Line a 20cm (8in) round tin with greaseproof paper.

3. Stir the ground almonds, nuts and beaten eggs into the fruit mixture and mix well. Sieve in the flour and mixed spice, stir well to integrate and transfer to the prepared tin. (If you have time, leaving the prepared mixture in the tin for a couple of hours before baking will result in a moister cake.) Bake the cake for 90 minutes, covering with greaseproof paper once it browns on the top to ensure it doesn't burn. The cake is cooked if an inserted skewer comes out clean. If not, you may need to continue cooking for another 30 minutes or more.

4. Once cooked, remove from the oven and when cool enough to handle, turn out onto a wire rack. Turn upside down and prick the base with a skewer, sprinkle the remaining alcohol over and allow to soak in. Once fully cooled, wrap well and store in a cool dark place for four weeks if possible. For an extra moist result, dab the cake with alcohol every week.

Marzipan & Royal Icing

You could serve your Christmas Cake without these finishing touches, but the effort of putting the icing on the cake rarely goes unappreciated.

for the marzipan
- 500g (1lb 2oz) ground almonds
- 500g (1lb 2oz) icing sugar
- 2 eggs, beaten
- ¼ lemon, juice only

for the royal icing
- 3 egg whites
- 500g (1lb 2oz) icing sugar
- 1 teaspoon glycerine

ICA Tip
If the icing on a cake goes so hard that it breaks when it's cut, you can dampen a clean cloth in cold water, wring It out and wrap the cake overnight before cutting.

1. To make the marzipan, empty the almonds into a large mixing bowl and sieve most of the sugar over, reserving a little for dusting a clean work surface. Add the beaten egg together with the lemon juice. Beat to a firm paste and transfer to the dusted surface to knead it into a workable texture.

2. To make the icing, lightly whisk the egg whites in a large mixing bowl, sieving in the icing sugar little by little as you whisk. Bring to the consistency of thick peaks, about 10 minutes, before folding in the glycerine and whisking a little further to integrate fully.

3. To cover the cake, begin with a thin layer of apricot jam thinned out with a little hot water, followed by a layer of marzipan which should be rolled out before attaching. The apricot glaze will help it to adhere to the cake.

4. Finish with a layer of icing, spread evenly with a spatula or warm palette knife. If achieving the smooth effect causes problems, make a virtue of your little peaks for a fresh snow effect. Any surplus icing can be piped on and the cake can be decorated with silver balls and green and red ribbon. Set aside overnight to dry and allow the icing to set, and store in an airtight tin until ready to serve.

Nollaig na mBan

Christmas is a wonderful time for all the family, with extended family coming home from foreign shores, the kids on holidays from school and some of us lucky enough to be on annual holidays from work. But someone's got to do all that extra cooking, not to mention clean the whole house before, during and after the big events scattered throughout the festive season. And that's before the shopping has been fitted in – for presents as well as a well-stocked larder. Traditionally, all of this was the domain of the Irish mammy. So it's just as well that she also traditionally got an official day off, under strict instructions to put the feet up and let someone else do all the running around.

The sixth of January is the Feast of the Epiphany in the Catholic calendar, marking the day the three wise men brought their gifts to the infant Jesus in the manger. In Ireland it is widely known as Little Christmas, and considered to be the last day of the Christmas season, when the Christmas tree and decorations are taken down and stored away. More work for the womenfolk, you might think, but this day also doubles up as Women's Christmas, a day of rest after such Trojan seasonal efforts. The tradition is strongest in the south-west of the country, but can and should be revived elsewhere. Breakfast in bed would be as good a place to start the day as any. After all, Christmas time is all about family traditions, and there's no harm in creating new ones as you go along!

Back in the Day...

"On the last day of Christmas, also known as Little Christmas or Nollaig na mBan (Women's Christmas), we always helped mother out with the chores of the day. We would make boxty in the little skillet pot on the turf fire while mother relaxed listening to her favourite programmes on the radio, Harbour Hotel and Dear Frankie."
Mary O'Neill, Wicklow

Boxty

ROCKCORRY GUILD MEMBERS, MONAGHAN

Boxty is a very traditional breakfast accompaniment and, if served with a full Irish fry, is a good way to ensure that a mid-morning breakfast keeps hungry appetites satisfied long into the day. But it can also make a nice accompaniment for a more modern Irish brunch, replacing a muffin or brioche in an Egg Florentine for example (with poached eggs, spinach, smoked salmon and Hollandaise sauce).

Serves 4–8

INGREDIENTS
- 250g (9oz) raw potato
- 250g (9oz) mashed potato
- 250g (9oz) plain flour
- 1 tablespoon bicarbonate of soda
- 1 tablespoon salt
- pepper (optional)
- 50g (2oz) butter, melted (you can use low fat butter)
- 125ml (4fl oz) milk

what you'll need
- linen tea towel

ICA Tip
A great way to use up leftover potatoes, boxty can also be made in advance and chilled until ready to cook. Just allow them to return to room temperature first so that they cook evenly.

1. Grate the raw potatoes into a large mixing bowl. Turn out onto a cloth and wring dry. Add the mashed potatoes and mix well to combine. Sieve in the dry ingredients, season with pepper to taste, and mix well with the melted butter to bind.

2. Add a little milk to make a pliable dough. Turn out onto a floured surface and knead lightly. Divide into four and shape to form large flat cakes. Mark each into quarters (but without cutting right through).

3. Heat a lightly greased griddle or heavy-based pan over a medium heat and cook the boxty for 10–15 minutes, or until golden and cooked through, turning halfway so that they colour evenly.

Cook a Full Irish Breakfast

1. Traditionally the full Irish breakfast contains the works: pork sausages and rashers from your local butcher, fresh blood black pudding and white pudding too, free-range eggs (preferably fresh from the yard outside), mushrooms and tomatoes. And traditionally all of this would be fried, right down to the white soda bread itself.

2. Timing is important as is keeping everything warm. Today you might want to stick on the oven to a lowish temperature and transfer the cooked foods to a baking tray to keep warm as you cook the rest. Start with the moister products such as sausages and pudding and vegetables. Leave the rashers to the end so that they don't dry out, followed by the eggs which can be cooked to order.

3. If you have the oven on as well as the stovetop, you might as well go the whole hog and use the grill for some of the cooking too. It'll speed the whole process up and your family's waistlines and hearts will thank you for what will be a considerably healthier start to the day. Everything bar the egg can be cooked under the grill instead of being fried. If you really want to keep things healthy, swap the fried egg for poached.

4. A good trick for a perfectly shaped poached egg without an egg poacher is to cover a mug loosely with clingfilm and push down a little to create a hollow into which you can break the egg. Lift this out, tie the clingfilm and drop it into a pan of simmering water to cook. Alternatively try placing a metal pastry cutter into the water and break the egg inside the cutter to help shape the poached egg. Adding a teaspoon of vinegar to the water will keep the pan clean and help the whites coagulate, while a teaspoon of salt will prevent the egg whites from toughening.

5. Don't forget about liquid refreshments too. Remember when making fresh coffee that just-boiled water will burn the coffee grains, so better to let it cool for a minute before brewing, while tea must be made with freshly boiled water. (See p172 for more tips on making the perfect cuppa.)

The Birthday Party

There's a lot to be thinking about for a child's birthday party, which is why it's sometimes best to just keep certain things as simple as possible. Both of these tried and tested birthday cakes are much loved by their respective families. And neither involve switching an oven on. Which is not to say that baking a birthday cake can't be great fun for those who love to bake (and you'll find lots of much-loved recipes for cakes and puddings in The ICA Cookbook). But it's good to remember that there's always another approach, and it doesn't have to involve buying someone else's creation.

The extra time you'll have on your hands can be used to organise some old-fashioned party games. You may be surprised how much the tech-savvy generation enjoys them.

Pass the Parcel is always a favourite, with its building excitement over what the prize might be and who will get it. The parcel is passed around until the music stops, when the child holding it can take off a layer of wrapping. You can have a bit of fun wrapping boxes within boxes to confound their expectations. Musical Chairs and Hot Potato are two variations of the same game: when the music stops, every child should aim to avoid being the odd one out, either as the only one not to be sitting on a chair or the one left holding the (figuratively) hot potato. Simon Says is fun to play with a younger group, or you could borrow some ideas from traditional Halloween games such as bobbing for apples, in which players must try to bite an apple in a basin of water – harder than it sounds!

No-Bake Ice-Cream Birthday Cake

MARGARET BOWKETT, WEXFORD

*This is a really quick and easy way to make a delightful children's birthday cake
which can be assembled minutes before serving. Children love the novelty
and it can be as economical or extravagant as you choose.*

Serves 12–15

INGREDIENTS
- 4 x 1-litre blocks of ice-cream
- 1 packet of chocolate fingers, halved lengthways
- 1 large bag of marshmallows
- 250g (½lb) mixed sweets (Smarties, chocolate buttons, dolly-mix etc)
- 6 chocolate flakes, crumbled into small pieces

what you'll need
- a large plate or tray covered in tin-foil
- birthday candles

1. Just before serving, place the four blocks of ice-cream together on a large plate or foil-wrapped tray to form a rectangle.

2. Place the halved chocolate fingers on each of the four corners and around the edge of your ice-cream blocks, spacing evenly to use all pieces. Place marshmallows in the spaces between the chocolate fingers.

3. Cover the top of the cake with your choice of mixed sweets and sprinkle the crumbled flake over the top (and around the sides if you wish) to fill in any gaps. Add your candles, serve promptly, and wait for the screams of delight.

No-Bake Chocolate Biscuit Cake

PAULINE O'CALLAGHAN, CORK

This has been the birthday cake used by Pauline for all her children and grandchildren's birthdays for the last forty years. It is ideal for children's parties and the logs can be cut into number shapes to represent the birthday age.

Serves 10–12

INGREDIENTS
- 175g (6oz) cooking chocolate
- 1 egg, separated
- 110g (4oz) icing sugar
- 85g (3oz) margarine
- 1 packet rectangular morning coffee biscuits
- 150ml (¼ pint) milk

ICA Tips
The biscuits needed for this cake can be a little hard to find in Ireland, although they're readily available in the UK. Pick up a few packets when you see them for sale as they keep well.

1. Place a heatproof bowl over a pot of boiling water to create a bain marie, break in the chocolate and allow it to melt. Meanwhile, separate the egg and whisk the white. Gently fold the whisked egg white into the melted chocolate (this will help take all the chocolate off the edge of the bowl).

2. In a separate large mixing bowl, beat the icing sugar, margarine and egg yolk together, add the melted chocolate, mix and blend well.

3. Spread five biscuits side by side on a serving plate to make the base of the cake of about 25cm (10in) in length. Cover the base with a layer of chocolate mixture, and then cover this with another layer of biscuits, first dipping these biscuits into the milk to soften. Repeat with another four or five layers of chocolate and biscuits.

4. Cover the top, sides and ends with the chocolate mixture and indent with the prongs of a fork to give a nice finish. Chill the cake in the fridge for at least an hour or for up to three or four days.

Chapter 5
The Garden

GROWING GREEN FINGERS • WORKING WITH MOTHER NATURE
UNWANTED VISITORS • GARDEN MAINTENANCE & SAFETY
DRESSING YOUR HOME

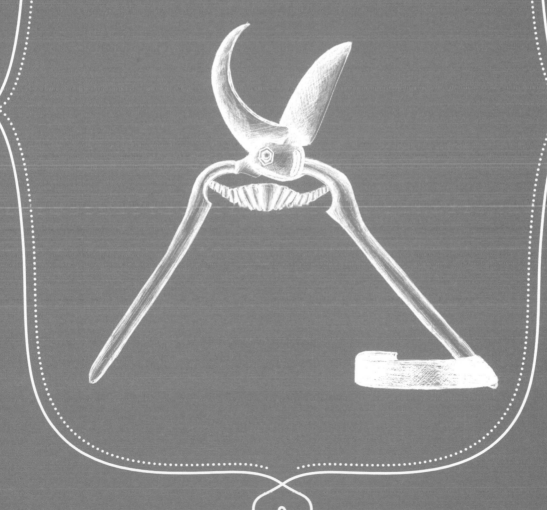

Growing Green Fingers

There is so much pleasure to be had from creating your own garden and so much potential in terms of extending the home outdoors. Whether you dream of living the good life and growing your own food to feed your family, or you simply want an oasis in which to unwind on one of our long Irish evenings, whatever time, money and energy you invest will be well returned.

A word of warning though. Gardens do take work – real physical graft – and it is easy to under-estimate the time and commitment which they will demand. Keep ambition in check and start modestly with a garden that is a manageable size. A good guide is to aim for one that you can dig yourself by hand. If you have to get a rotovator or someone else in to dig your garden because of lack of time or energy, you probably won't have the time or energy to maintain it later in the year either. Better to grow your plants, flowers and vegetables in a few well-maintained raised beds and containers than to have a sprawling messy garden that reproaches you every time you go out the door.

If you're a novice in the garden, take the time to talk to people who aren't. Ask local gardeners about which vegetables, plants and trees grow well in the area. Local knowledge can save you a lot of trial and error, and people are happy to share their experience. Besides, gardeners often have lots of seedlings and rooted cuttings that they are only too happy to share with a fellow gardening enthusiast. If you wish to grow from seed yourself, be sure to buy decent seed. Cheap seed often germinates poorly and as a result the plants are often poor too.

> *If you have loads of seeds left after planting, why not organise a seed-swop tea party to share seeds and young plants with friends and neighbours?*
> Theresa Storey, Limerick

The Gardener's Pleasure
My perky little Aconite,
A picture to behold
Bravely peeping through the snow
In winter's biting cold.

Each delicate wee petal
Has a very special way
Of spreading rays of sunshine
On my grey and dullest day.

Although it may seem fragile
It really is quite bold
As together with its roots and stem
It has a heart of gold.

So if the days of winter
Are as dreary as I'm told
I only need to look at it
And beauty will enfold.

Connie McEvoy, Louth

114

Mind the Pennies...
"Use old tights for tying stakes to shrubs
and delicate plants."
Kathleen Murray, Dublin

Get Started

1. If you see a plant or flower that you like, ask the owner's permission to take a cutting. Always take three slips with heels and one will surely grow.

2. To keep cuttings fresh while travelling, stick the cut end into a raw potato and they will stay hydrated until you get home.

3. Egg cartons filled with compost are ideal for growing seeds and garlic bulbs, as are the cardboard inserts from toilet rolls. When the shoots are ready for planting, just pop the entire thing into the soil in your garden or raised bed. The roots will not be disturbed and the cardboard will compost down into the soil.

4. Some seeds need a little kick-start to wake them up. Before sowing parsley seeds, pour boiling water over them to accelerate germination.

5. Newly sown seeds are delicate creatures. To water without disturbing them, gently squeeze over some drops of water from a soaked cotton-wool ball. Eyebrow tweezers are useful for removing weeds from pots containing fragile plants and seedlings.

6. Banana peel makes an excellent natural fertiliser. Chop it into small pieces and scatter these in the hole before planting new plants. Tomato feed is ideal for any flowering plant.

7. An armful of nettles soaked in rainwater for a fortnight makes a smelly but efficient liquid fertiliser which is high in potash and particularly suited for use on tomatoes.

8. When growing plants in pots rather than groundsoil, keep an eye on the pot's base for roots peeking out – a sign that the plant has outgrown it. Transfer to a new pot one size up, filled with compost and a slow fertiliser.

9. It can be hard to remember what you planted where. Paint a square of blackboard paint onto your garden pots and chalk on plant names, notes to self or anything you fancy. Recycled lollipop sticks are handy for popping into soil beds as home-made signposts.

10. Willow contains vast amounts of plant rooting hormones. To harness these, soak some willow twigs in a bucket of water for 24 hours. Immerse plant or shrub cuttings in this willow tea for several hours before planting, or water newly planted cuttings with the willow tea to help them root.

Gifting Plants

A pretty houseplant can make a lovely gift, but it's worth considering if you want to give something with a short season's lifespan or if you'd rather present someone with a gift that keeps on giving and giving. Hyacinths can be bought in early spring while in flower or just about to – they are very affordable and give a beautiful scent, but their season is short. Christmas cacti on the other hand will last for up to ten years, and will continue to flower every year. They are a handy plant to grow from a cutting in February or March. Simply cut three leaves from a branch and place the cut end into potting soil. Feed with Baby Bio and water every six days for a month, and then tend as needed. Don't overlook evergreen plants which can last for many years. Bear in mind too that some of us have greener fingers than others. Orchids for example are very striking but are susceptible to draughts and easily killed off (although once they find a warm spot they like they can thrive). Plants that have been produced locally will be more durable than those imported from warmer climes.

Growing Your Own Food

People have returned to growing their own food again. Some are concerned about the overload of chemical fertilisers and pesticides in many commercially bought fruits and vegetables. Others are attracted to the nostalgia of age-old practices, or wish to reconnect with the food we put on our plates. Nothing beats sitting out on a warm evening surrounded by summer flowers, enjoying some nice home-grown salads.

Growing your own food is attractive to many people for many reasons. However, it is easy to get carried away in spring thinking this will be the year you will become self-sufficient in vegetables. Stop for a minute and think. Instead of wasting your limited time on vegetables such as carrots and potatoes which are affordable and readily available, consider growing peas and beans, spinach and greens, heirloom varieties of tomatoes and unusual oriental vegetables. Have a look in a seed catalogue to browse the possibilities.

Grow vegetables you will look forward to eating. Don't grow vegetables that you don't actually like just because you think you should (or your father-in-law thinks you should!) or because they grow well in the garden. It's up to you whether you plant from seeds, but if you only want a few plants of anything like tomatoes or courgette consider just buying the plants. It will save you struggling to re-home lots of unwanted seedlings.

Starting small can bring great satisfaction too. Salads and small vegetables can be grown in pots or grow bags. Sew lettuce, scallions and radish, and you have the makings of a fresh, healthy salad. The beauty of salad leaves is that you can simply harvest what you need as you need it. Little Gem or Tom Thumb lettuce are good varieties to try, and look for White Lisbon scallions. Carrots grow well in small containers (look out for the Early Nante variety) and potatoes can be grown in deep pots, containers or barrels. Tomatoes are sometimes grown in pots or growbags (Balconi Collection or Garden Pearl both make good varieties to try), but can also be grown in hanging baskets. They can be sown as seed inside on the windowsill. The key is to choose a sheltered spot that gets good sunshine. Sowing marigold amongst them helps to keep away whitefly (see opposite).

Back in the Day...

"When I was growing up, our family didn't have a garden or farm from which to be self-sufficient, but we were never short of spuds, vegetables or milk. My father would hire a few acres every year from a local farmer where he would sow enough potatoes, cabbage and turnips to get us through the year. The harvested potatoes would be 'pitted' for the winter: packed into a pit insulated with layers of straw to keep out the frost and help preserve them. He also had a crop of hay from this land.

We had a cow on the 'long acre', which meant that every day after the morning milking, the cow would be let out to wander and graze along the roadside. In the evening my mother would hop on her bike to find the cow and bring her home for milking. She would be kept overnight in the back yard. My father would barter with other neighbours, swapping milk and spuds for other fruit and veg we did not have. I always thought that it was an ingenious way of working as we had no land ourselves but we still had the best of fruit, veg and milk. It is beginning to look like we could return to that way of living in today's world."

Norah McDermott, Kildare

Complementary Plants

Some plants will help others grow by protecting them from disease or pests or boosting them in other ways. For example, the roots of spinach secrete a growth-enhancing hormone into the surrounding soil, making spinach an excellent companion plant for broccoli.

French marigolds are more than just pretty to look at. When planted through the garden, they exude a chemical through their roots that deters soil-borne pests such as nematodes and whitefly. On the other hand, flying insects such as aphids are attracted to yellow flowers. Planting some yellow marigolds downwind of your valuable plants makes it hard for the pests to fly upwind to get to them. The Tagetes Minuta variety of marigold is used by some gardeners to curtail the spread of bindweed, couch grass and ground elder.

Rose bushes – yellow ones in particular – are very susceptible to black spot, which is typically treated with a copper-containing fungicide. An alternative is to make up a solution of three teaspoons of bicarbonate of soda and one teaspoon of fertiliser in a jam jar of water with a squirt of washing-up liquid, shake up well and spray onto the plants. However, lavender, rosemary and mint all contain natural anti-fungal essential oils which can help prevent black spot when planted under rose bushes. Lavender may also stop aphids from attacking rose bushes. Planting garlic among roses strengthens resistance to disease and will help to keep the greenfly away.

Invest in a Polytunnel

If you're serious about growing your own food, do yourself a favour and buy a polytunnel. The weather is too poor here in Ireland to work without one. Not only will it extend the growing season at both ends, allowing you to harvest salad greens and herbs in the darkest depths of winter, but polytunnels are so warm and sheltered that they make gardening in bad weather a joy. Invest in the biggest one you can afford, and consider stringing up a hammock to really take advantage of the balmy micro-climate you'll be creating.

> " My mother always told us to never take goodness from the soil without returning it. "
> Breda McDonald, Kilkenny

Keeping Chickens

With the price of real free-range eggs going up and up, it's only sensible to keep chickens if you can. They are very economical to rear and even a very small garden can support a few hens. They make excellent pet animals and are good companions.

Chickens need lots of clean water; during the summer months, place the water feeder in the shade to keep it cool. They will eat kitchen scraps, cooked food, vegetables and some garden waste and you can supplement their feed with commercial chicken food to ensure a balanced diet. If you leave them wandering freely, they will get a large proportion of their food from foraging. Be warned though: they will scratch up your garden plants and will love to take dust baths in your large plant pots.

You can buy some lovely chicken houses nowadays in all sorts of colours, shapes and sizes, but virtually any shed or outbuilding can be converted into a chicken house. Free-range hens will only sleep and lay eggs in their chicken house so it doesn't need to be fancy. However, it does need to be insulated and ventilated: cool in summer, warm in winter. The basic requirements will be perches for the birds to sleep on, food and water dishes, and nest boxes to lay eggs in. The chicken house must also be animal-proof to prevent rats, foxes, stoats and even dogs from accessing and stealing food, eggs and the birds themselves. You can let your hens roam freely around the garden during the day or keep them in a pen, thus keeping them away from your prized plants and protecting them from predators.

A word of warning. We often see charming pictures in gardening books of chickens happily scratching between vegetables in a garden and hear people talk about keeping their chickens in the vegetable patch. More likely is that the hens will go through the garden like a horde of locusts, eating everything and then scratching up the ground to make themselves dust baths. Do keep that in mind if you are considering pursuing the self-sufficiency dream.

Choose Your Chickens

1. When buying your hens, the choice is between pure-breed, hybrid or bantam.

2. For the regular person who just wants a few hens for a personal supply of eggs, hybrids such as classic red hens are recommended. These are readily available at about half the price of pure-breeds, are reliable layers and are fairly unfussy.

3. To find where to buy your hens, check the classified ads, ask other hen owners, browse the internet or go to your local markets.

4. Some animal welfare societies have rescue hens they need to re-home. At about a year old, these ex-battery farm hens are past their prime egg-laying period and would have been destined to be killed. They will still lay eggs, just not as many as a commercial grower wants, and they would appreciate a good home.

5. Only buy clean, alert, healthy-looking hens with full feathers and bright eyes. Pay attention to the conditions in which they are kept. Healthy hens come from clean, airy, well-lit homes.

6. Ask the seller what food they have been feeding them: you don't want to change their diet too drastically. Most sellers will give you a small bag of their food to take home with you.

7. Hens are quite happy without a cockerel – there is no need to get one and your neighbours won't thank you if you do.

8. Buy your hens when they are at least 16 weeks old. Any younger than that makes it very hard to tell what sex the chicken is, and you don't want to end up with a bunch of cockerels. The chicken seller may assure you they are all hens, but buyer beware!

9. Hens can catch colds, pick up worms from wild birds and get a few other diseases but, for the most part, they are really very easy to keep.

10. If you have queries, go to your local veterinary supply shop who will provide any medicines you might need and answer any questions you might have.

Back in the Day...

"The American Bronze turkeys were the bane of my childhood existence on my parent's farm. Dodging the wicked turkey cock every time I went to fetch a bucket of water from the well at the far end of the haggard was an essential art, as he was wont to fly at and peck or scratch anyone who was unfortunate enough to cross his path. My siblings and I were terrified of him but he never attacked my father, so he would regularly escort us on our way.

In springtime when the hens started to 'lie' (an indication that they would soon start laying eggs and needed the cock to thread them so as the eggs would be fertile), they would just flop down in front of me without warning, causing me to trip and spill their water or break the eggs that I had carefully collected in my apron from their nests.

The worst indignity of all was when a hen had laid for two weeks running. I would be instructed to take her to another turkey cock – usually at the other end of the parish – just in case ours was infertile. Usually, two hens were taken at a time in a cardboard box perched on the back carrier of the bike. Imagine the remarks passed and questions asked by farmer's sons who were usually laying or coppicing hedges along roads and lanes or yeaning ewes in the fields. Such excursions weren't forgotten until the next dance attended. The first question asked when tripping the light fantastic was less likely to be 'do you come here often?' than 'did you have to use a saddle?' (in reference to the saddles used when a wicked turkey cock trampled on and tore the back of a hen that he was about to thread).

The eggs were stored in tea chests half-filled with bran until the hens were ready to cover a sitting. This would be announced by a hen refusing to leave the nest after laying an egg. Under cover of night's darkness, a clutch (usually 12 or 13 eggs) would be carefully placed under her. It took a full month for them to hatch but after ten days, eggs were tested for fertility. This was done in the dark using a flash lamp which was held underneath the egg. Clear eggs were deemed to be infertile and taken away. There was a great excitement to see the clouded outline of a little turkey beginning to develop in the fertile eggs. My mother always said, 'Come on now and we will say a prayer after the rosary that there will be no thunder or blasting in the nearby quarry until after they're hatched.' The noise would kill the unhatched chicks.

Once a clutch was hatched, the hatchlings were fed a special recipe for the first three days of their existence. Two eggs would be scrambled up with a quarter mug of milk, a knob of farm butter and a dessertspoon each of chopped dandelion leaves and nettle leaves. I can tell you that it tasted delicious and having cooked it three times a day for three days, I always enjoyed the first spoonful before allowing the wee turkeys to peck it from my fingers. Later they moved on to mash or ration.

When they got old enough, they loved to perch in the highest trees in the haggard and I got cruel hardship trying to get them down and in before dark. And as you have probably guessed, the young cocks were getting wicked by now and so the cycle began again." *Connie McEvoy, Louth*

124

Working with Mother Nature

There are several ways you can harness the potential of Mother Nature, from making your own natural fertilisers and pest deterrents to home composting and even building your own wormery.

Composting a household's organic waste ticks several boxes. It is more eco-friendly than throwing compostables into a landfill site. It reduces refuse bills as organic material generally makes up at least one quarter of a typical household's waste. And by producing your own, you have a free source of compost to use to pot up plants or as a soil conditioner.

Simple Home Composting

Creating a home compost heap couldn't be simpler, being nothing more than a pile of vegetable and organic waste left to decompose naturally with the aid of bacteria and other micro-organisms. The resulting compost is blackish brown and crumbly in texture and can be used by gardeners to improve all types of soil, whether clayey, silty or sandy. However, regular compost is not very nutritious so you will still need to use a fertiliser to feed your plants.

All of this organic material breaking down is not the tidiest thing to look at, which is why most of us use a ready-made compost bin or build a contained space which can hold the decaying material until it's ready to use. Compost bins are readily available in garden centres or supermarkets, and many county councils sell them cheaply or even give them away.

Site your compost heap in a sheltered, sunny spot that is quick and easy to access from the kitchen. The warmer the heap is maintained, the faster it will compost. Place the base-less bin directly onto bare soil to allow the soil's micro-organisms and worms to gain access to the compost inside. Fill the bins with fresh waste from the top through the removable lid and as the material turns to compost, remove it using the low door on the front of the bin.

Chicken wire on stakes, bales of straw, breeze blocks, old metal drums and concrete can all be fashioned into a home-made compost bin. Old wooden pallets wired together into a square gives quite a large bin which will last up to five years. The disadvantage of a home-made bin is that the compost can't be easily removed as it is made. The answer is to keep two rotating bins on the go; one can be filled up as the other is composting down.

What to Compost?

GARDEN WASTE: Leaves, green weeds, vegetable debris (such as rhubarb leaves and cabbage stalks), rotted straw, old potting soil and dead plants, grass cuttings and woody shrub prunings (no more than pencil-thick though). Cut nettles and non-flowering thistle tops are a great source of nutritious green material for the heap.

HOUSEHOLD & KITCHEN WASTE: Keep a bucket in the kitchen for vegetable scraps, egg shells, tea leaves and bags, coffee grounds and dead flower arrangements. You can also add hair from hair brushes, vacuum cleaner waste and tumble dryer lint. Also add paper, including old envelopes, sugar bags, paper bags, newspapers – any non-glossy paper that has been shredded.

ANIMAL & BIRD MANURE: The bedding from your chicken house can go straight onto the compost heap.

SEAWEED: Bring back a couple of bucketfuls from the beach to add valuable trace minerals.

AVOID: Cooked food will attract rodents while pet waste or cat litter pose health risks. Disease spoors from diseased plants or vegetables may live in your compost heap and infect next year's plants. Perennial weeds such as bindweed and dock or couch grass should not be added, nor plants that have gone to seed.

Maintaining Your Compost

Before filling your bin, place a few wooden sticks at the bottom to allow a little air to circulate and aid decomposition. When adding organic waste, an ideal ratio is two parts brown woody material to one part green leafy and manure material, but treat this as a rough guide. A well-mixed combination is better than separate layers of matter. If you are feeling energetic you can speed up the decomposition by periodically emptying out the bin and mixing well to aerate before refilling. A few spades worth of old compost and garden soil added to the heap introduces extra micro-organisms to the compost.

Keep the heap damp but not soaking to encourage the micro-organisms to flourish. The heap should be well covered in very wet weather. Once the material reaches the top of the bin, cover with a breathable cover such as perforated plastic, sacks, straw or an old carpet and leave the mixture to break down until it turns into lovely crumbly compost. Depending on weather and time of year, this can take anything from a couple of months to a year.

Worm Composting

Worm composting produces both a fine, crumbly compost that is considerably more nutritious than regular compost (one part worm compost to three or four parts soil making an excellent potting soil mix) and also a highly nutritious liquid fertiliser. This liquid gold should be collected through the drainage holes, diluted to the colour of weak green tea and used for watering your plants.

You can add all cooked food including meat scraps, which cuts down kitchen wastage and refuse costs considerably. Avoid citrus peel and spices as these contain antimicrobial essential oils which counteract the helpful micro-organisms. Worms work best between 18°C–25°C and stop working at temperatures below 10°C so they would need a bit of insulation here if kept outdoors during an Irish winter.

The bins are readily available and can be stored indoors, outdoors or in a frost-proof shed (some neat little ones double up as coffee tables), or you could make your own from a strong waterproof container drilled with holes for ventilation and drainage. The red-striped 'tiger worms' can also be bought from suppliers or gathered from under piles of leaf mould, manure heaps or compost. You will need about one hundred worms to start your colony.

In the base of the worm bin, combine some damp shredded black-and-white newspaper with equal parts leaf mould to home-made compost or manure and a little garden soil. Add the worms and some kitchen waste, cover with damp newspaper and leave for a few days. Begin by adding small amounts of food waste to avoid overloading the worms and bury any cooked food under other waste so it doesn't attract flies. Continue feeding the worms until the bin is full and keep the compost moist but not waterlogged. Once settled in, the worms will start to breed and produce little grain-like cocoons. To empty the bin, remove the top few worm-heavy inches of compost. Set this aside in order to recolonise the bin and empty out the rest of the compost.

Natural Fertilisers

Even if you don't go as far as composting, there are lots of simple uses for everyday household waste. Used teabags can be used to line your flowerpots and baskets, where they will both feed the plants and help to conserve water. Ash from a wood-burning stove is full of potash, and can be scattered onto shrubs and other garden plants, while soot from a regular chimney can be sprayed onto fruit trees in springtime to keep disease at bay.

Egg shells make a great fertiliser for potted plants. Collect the empty egg shells in a container, top up with water, cover and leave for a week before pouring over your outdoor plants. Admittedly the odour can be pretty unpleasant, but your plants will thank you for the feed.

Bananas are full of potassium which can help your roses to flourish, increasing both the number and size of blooms; simply cut up the peel and overripe banana flesh and scatter around the base of your rosebushes.

Nettle's extensive root systems absorb lots of nutrients which then accumulate in the nettle stems and leaves, making for an excellent home-made fertiliser. To make up a nettle tea for your garden plants, soak the stems and leaves in a bucket of water for a few weeks until the water starts to turn tea-coloured. Water your plants regularly with this liquid, diluting it until it is the colour of weak green tea. Sickly plants can be given a pick-me-up with a drink of a cooled pot of chamomile tea. Alternatively plant chamomile throughout the garden to keep everything in good health.

Give acid-loving plants like azaleas, rhododendrons, hydrangeas and gardenias a little boost by watering them with a white distilled vinegar solution (a cupful of vinegar to a gallon of water). The acidic vinegar will help to release iron in the soil. Pouring the solution directly over your azaleas will also give the leaves a lovely sheen.

A Year in the Kitchen Garden

MARCH

The first early potatoes can be sown in mid-March, although waiting until April is a safer option. Spray chimney soot onto fruit trees to keep disease at bay. Seeds can be sown indoors on sunny windowsills.

APRIL

Sow cabbages, cauliflower, Brussels sprouts, carrots and parsnips early in the month.

MAY

Sow main-crop peas and beans, and thin out carrots and parsnips. Hold off planting out your summer bedding until May or you risk losing them to a late frost.

JUNE

Continue sowing beetroot, turnips and salads. Keep pinching side shoots from tomatoes. As the temperature gets warmer, weeds will become a problem so do try and keep on top of them. The most useful tool in the garden is a hoe for weeding.

JULY

The warmer weather means a lot of watering and weeding are needed. Potato blight can be a problem, and it can also affect tomatoes.

AUGUST

Sow spring cabbages and scallions.

SEPTEMBER

Enjoy your harvest of home-produced potatoes and vegetables. If you have a surplus be sure to store them well. Cooking apples should be picked when dry and stored in a cool dry place inside cardboard boxes layered with newspaper to ensure they are not touching.

OCTOBER

Collect autumn leaves in a refuse bag, make a few holes in the bottom, water and tie. By next autumn you'll have your own leaf mould for mulching.

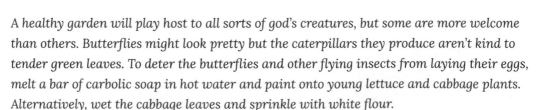

Unwanted Visitors

A healthy garden will play host to all sorts of god's creatures, but some are more welcome than others. Butterflies might look pretty but the caterpillars they produce aren't kind to tender green leaves. To deter the butterflies and other flying insects from laying their eggs, melt a bar of carbolic soap in hot water and paint onto young lettuce and cabbage plants. Alternatively, wet the cabbage leaves and sprinkle with white flour.

If ants are a particular problem, the most effective approach is to mix borax powder with sugar and scatter it near the nest. However, this poisonous mixture is also dangerous to children and pets, so you may want to seek a gentler method. Try wiping down the affected area with a solution of equal parts vinegar and water, and spray the solution around doors and window frames and other ant trails. Cracks in the walls can be sealed with a little petroleum jelly. Cinnamon and mint are both good natural deterrents, as is drawing a line of chalk across the ants' preferred routes.

Rabbits are unlikely to be a problem in an urban garden, but if you do need to protect your plants from wild rabbits, place cotton wool balls soaked in vinegar in an old film container. Poke a hole into the top and place in the garden. Alternatively human hair, available from your hairdresser, will keep rabbits at bay as they will not cross it.

Back in the Day…

"My dad and I used to collect the used twine from bales of hay and use it to string together empty tin cans to be hung over the cabbages and lettuce. There was not a crow or pigeon in sight."
Betty Gorman, Laois

Slugs

Slugs can do a lot of damage to freshly sown young plants in just one night's raid. If you don't want to use chemical heavy slug pellets, there are several natural approaches to controlling slugs, although these methods are by no means fully effective and are not for the squeamish.

One labour-intensive approach is to collect the slugs by hand in a wide-bottomed, salt-lined bucket (at dusk or later in the night with a torch), or to skip the salt and either spray them with a solution of equal parts water and vinegar or simply scald them with boiling water to kill them. Dispose of the remains in the compost heap or bury them in the garden. (Excessive salt is not good for the garden, so stick to one burial area if using.)

A more ghoulish method is to head into the garden armed with a torch and long-bladed scissors, and chop the slugs in half. You can leave these unsalted slugs for the birds to dispose of. The birds will also help deal with slug eggs. When digging the garden, if you come across a cluster of pearl-like eggs, simply leave them exposed for the birds to polish off.

If life is too short to spend an evening picking off slugs individually, try leaving an upturned, scooped-out grapefruit or melon half in the garden. The slugs will congregate under the shell during the night, and can then be dealt with as above. Or fill a shallow tray with beer to which slugs are attracted, but in which they will drown.

Another popular approach is to place slices of cucumber into an aluminium dish left in your garden, greenhouse or polytunnel. Chemicals in the cucumber react with the aluminium to give off a subtle scent that is harmless to humans but offensive to insects and slugs. Likewise, slugs will keep away from a row of copper wire about four inches below the top of a raised bed.

Aside from killing them off, remember that slugs love damp piles of garden rubbish, so keeping the garden clean and dispatching any debris immediately will help cut down the slug population. Cover the sides of window boxes and plant pots with petroleum jelly to prevent slugs accessing the plants.

Garden Maintenance & Safety

Weed Control

Weeding mightn't be the most interesting part of gardening but it's important to stay on top of it. If things have gotten very out of control, you may need to take drastic measures. Starving weeds of light will kill an infestation within a year. Old pieces of carpet, sheets of cardboard or black polythene all do the job admirably.

Better that it doesn't come to that. Where possible, dig out dandelions before they flower or they will take over your lawn. To permanently remove dandelions, cut off the foliage to expose the root-tops and smother these with salt. Salt can also be sprinkled directly onto thistles to banish them.

Moss can become very slippery when wet, making it dangerous as well as unsightly. An eggcup of Jeyes Fluid mixed with two gallons of water will kill off moss and other kinds of fungal growth when sprayed on tarmac surfaces. Alternatively, sprinkle cheap washing powder directly onto moss during a dry spell, and leave for a week or two before sweeping up. For a weed-free driveway, sprinkle dry table salt or heavily salted boiling water directly onto grass and weeds growing between the cracks on pathways and crevices of brickwork. A dose of vinegar can also be effective in killing weeds, although you may need to repeat on new growth several times until the weeds stop reappearing.

Garden Safety

A well-maintained garden should be a safe haven for all the family, so make sure that there are no avoidable hazards, particularly for children and pets. If your garden is near a busy roadside, ensure that all boundaries are properly child-proofed, and teach children never to eat any plants in the garden so that they avoid poisonous ones such as laburnum.

Always put away garden tools correctly. You can make a protective sheath for sharp blades such as saws by recycling old garden hoses. When storing away tools like spades, rakes and hoes over the winter, clean well and push the blades deep into a bucket of fine dry sand to prevent rust. It is important to clean and service the lawnmower both before and after winter storage.

Garden Features & Furniture

Gardening can be a dirty business but there are a few shortcuts to keeping your garden clean and tidy. The crusty rim deposits and staining that occur in glazed clay and plastic flower pots and their saucers come right out without scrubbing. Just fill a sink or bucket with two parts cold water to one part vinegar, and soak the pots and saucers for about an hour or until they look clean and new. Wash with soap and water before re-using. To shift mould from terracotta pots, soak them in a solution of a cupful each of vinegar and bleach to one gallon of warm water. The mould should now scrub off with a steel wool pad.

Solid bird feeders and birdbaths are better scrubbed with neat vinegar than with cleaning soap or detergent, which can leave harmful residues. Rinse well afterwards. You can make your own

feeders from recycled netting (the kind you buy your onions in). Fill with nuts and bread and hang on trees using old shower curtain hooks.

If you've built your own fish pond, you'll need to treat the cement before adding fish and plants. Soak for a few days with a weak solution of water and vinegar, empty and rinse well before refilling.

Dressing Your Home

Window Boxes & Hanging Baskets

An afternoon spent planting up some window boxes or hanging baskets can bring many weeks' worth of pleasure, and makes for a thoughtful and affordable house-warming gift for others too.

While flowers in containers can dry out quickly and need regular watering – up to twice daily in hot weather – there is usually more of a danger of over-watering and drowning the plants. Always water bottom up (allowing the plant to soak up what water it needs) rather than top down, which can wash away important nutrients as well as risk drowning the roots. Window boxes, pots and containers all need drainage holes at the bottom and small stones or slate placed under the soil to allow for drainage. Choose a window box that is suitable for your window sill; it must be secure and able to bear the weight of soil and plants.

Hanging baskets can bring real cheer to a home's exterior. Trailing plants and those that produce lots of blooms on short stems are most suitable, mixed with some foliage for extra coverage. Choose as large a basket as the situation allows, and plant it densely so that the liner is not visible. Before filling the basket, cut holes around the sides of the liner into which you can insert the plants. Fill the basket with compost, moisture granules and fertiliser, and then place the plants through the holes at the side. Remember that it takes a couple of weeks for the basket to develop, and it might be advisable to keep it sheltered while the plants get established and settle in and before hanging it in its final position.

For spring displays, opt for evergreens and skimmias and fill gaps with small bulbs, tulips, daffodils and some colourful pansies. For summer blooms, try trailing petunias, geraniums, begonias and busy lizzies. Dahlias and some colourful lobelia can also be used. Remember that most flowers benefit from regular dead-heading (removing the spent flower heads) to keep them flowering throughout the season.

Over-Wintering Geraniums

Unlike many other flowering plants, geraniums can keep going for many years, re-blooming every year. They are pretty hardy, but if you don't want to leave them vulnerable to winter frost you could over-winter them in the traditional way. Lift the plants from the pot or ground before the first frost. Shake off as much soil as possible and trim the roots back to a couple of inches. Remove all the leaves and shorten the all-over length to four inches. Transfer to large trays about six inches deep, cover with a mixture of peat and sand and store in a frost-proof shed.

Healthy Houseplants

Houseplants need to be both fed and watered. Cold tea is excellent for indoor plants, as is the water used to boil your morning's egg. If you have an aquarium or fish bowl, save the water each time you change it and use it to water your house plants. You'll be amazed at the results.

If you don't have a helpful friend or neighbour to water plants while you're away for holidays, there are a few clever tricks to help keeping them watered without drowning the roots. Try standing the plants on a couple of planks of wood over the bath or a large sink full of water, and run lengths of wool from the water through the pot drainage hole to the soil. Alternatively, place the plants into the bath on thickly folded towels soaked in a few centimetres of water and they should look after themselves.

Bringing the Outdoors In

Spring bulbs such as snowdrops, muscari or daffodils need good drainage and can be challenging to raise indoors in pots. One trick is to plant them outside in the main beds, and dig them up just as they are coming into flower to plant them into bowls in the house. You can replant them back into the garden once they have flowered.

You can also bring the outdoors in by saving the heads of flowers such as hydrangeas, hanging them up to dry and then spraying them with silver or gold paint. During the autumn when beech leaves are at their most brilliant, cut some branches to keep. Stand them in a couple of inches of a mixture of half glycerine, half water. When all this liquid has been absorbed, the branches can be arranged in a dry vase to make a decoration that will last through the winter.

Keep Cut Flowers

1. Flowers are best cut from the garden in the late evening or early morning when they are less thirsty. Use a sharp garden scissors or shears, and plunge directly into a jug of water. Holding the stems under water, cut them diagonally and keep immersed while they take a good drink before transferring to a vase.

2. All cut flowers will keep longer if the vase is half-filled with a solution of one teaspoon of vinegar or bleach and one teaspoon of sugar to every 570ml (1 pint) of hot water. This also slows down the smelly slime which can appear on cut flower stems. Be sure to remove extra foliage from the lower stems so as not to over-crowd the water.

3. To revive cut flowers which have drooped, plunge the end of the stems into boiling water. By the time the water has cooled, the flowers will have perked up perfectly. Trim the stems and place in fresh cold water. This method helps extend the life of cut roses in particular.

4. Tulips can sometimes offer a very fleeting pleasure. Adding a drop of candlewax to the centre of cut tulips or a coin in the base of the vase can prevent them opening too quickly. A pin prick in the stem just below the flower also helps to keep them upright in their vase. Carnations last longer if placed in fizzy lemonade, while daffodils added to a mixed vase of flowers will emit a toxin that is harmful to the other flowers.

5. Glass vases can be difficult to clean. To remove very stubborn stains, fill with water and drop in two Alka Seltzer tablets, or add a mixture of vinegar and sea salt. The salt cleans the surface of the glass while the vinegar breaks down deposits. Neat vinegar will shift green slime and watermarks from vases: leave to soak for 10 minutes and then finish the job with a brush if you can reach inside. Alternatively, shake some rice or sand vigorously in the vase to loosen stubborn stains. Rinse well and dry thoroughly before storing.

Chapter 6

Home-made
Presents

IT'S THE THOUGHT • GET CRAFTY • GET COOKING

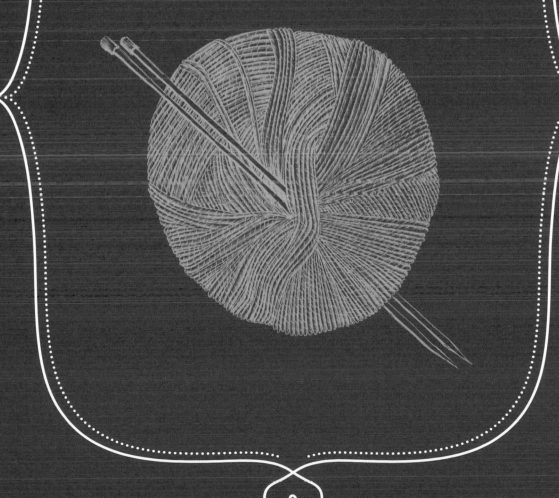

It's the Thought

Whether you want to make your own presents because you have little extra money to spare, or because you have a little extra time on your hands, whatever time you do invest is always greatly appreciated. There are so many thoughtful ways to make someone feel special, and some of them really do cost nothing but time.

Home-made Gifts

It could be as simple as filling a couple of plant pots with indoor plants grown from your own cuttings. This would make a lovely gift to brighten up a new home for someone, especially if they don't have naturally green fingers themselves – just be sure to include a little note with simple instructions for watering and light requirements (see p118 for more advice on gifting plants).

Think about ways to reframe precious memories and create new ones. You could stitch together a quilt for someone from their old sports jerseys or wornout t-shirts, allowing them to keep those memories close forever. Or make up several copies of a family recipe book which you can give to every family member, young and old alike. Simply gather together your family's best-loved recipes, whether from handwritten notes or old newspaper clippings passed down through generations or from a well-thumbed cookbook. Scan these together with some family photos and paste into a book or photo album to create a family treasure that will give years of pleasure. Include a family tree in the recipe book, or create a photo montage at the heart of a framed family tree to hang on the kitchen wall.

Sometimes what people really need is the encouragement to take time out or spend it in a particular way. Why not give a busy parent the gift of time to themselves? Offer to babysit and send them packing with a personalised parcel containing bath salts, candles, a trashy novel and chocolate. Or you could put together the makings of a sewing basket, complete with a pretty thimble and coloured threads for a teenage girl, or make up a wreath of fresh hardy herbs for a college student to hang in their kitchen. As the herbs dry, they can use them to flavour their pasta sauces (see p140 for more wreath ideas).

A little bit of anything can go a long way if it's beautifully wrapped, so get into the habit of recycling pretty wrapping paper, tissue paper, cellophane and brightly coloured leftover wallpaper, along with ribbons and bows and even the little ties from the shoulders of jumpers and blouses. Recycled baskets and shoeboxes can be used to make up your own personalised hampers, filled with all sorts home-made goodies. You could even transform your children's drawings into personalised Christmas cards. Apply a coating of hairspray to act as a fixative, strengthen the paper and prevent the colours from fading and rubbing off.

Make Your Own Wreaths

1. You can use garden prunings to create home-made wreaths. To test if the branches are suitable, twist them around your wrist: if the branches don't split they are pliable enough to weave into a wreath. Twist pencil- or finger-thick branches into a circle and wire them into shape, adding more branches and building up the thickness until you have a ready-to-dress wreath.

2. Willow or dogwood both make excellent rustic wreaths, as do prunings from other shrubs and small trees. Hornbeam is readily available and has a lovely silver, fissured bark. Willow can be turned into cuttings and planted after the wreath has been taken down, making it a double present.

3. Remember that wreaths aren't just for Christmas. You could make one for any occasion, dressing it as appropriate: hearts and roses for Valentine's Day; chicks, eggs and bunnies for Easter; or black roses and skeletons for a spooky Halloween wreath. Experiment with fresh flowers throughout the summer and with autumn leaves, dried flowers and berries later in the year.

4. Set aside a box especially for wreath dressing and fill it with decorations collected throughout the year (the seasonal sales make great hunting grounds). Try weaving through some battery-operated fairy lights in different shapes and colours, and use up scrap fabric and wool to make a big bow and little fabric and wool decorations. Raffia is excellent to use in wreaths instead of cloth ribbon: it is inexpensive, looks good and holds up well against the weather.

5. Dried berries and dried flowers such as hydrangea, statice and teasels make excellent indoor wreaths. Faded and pale dried flowers can be sprayed silver or gold before being added to the arrangement. Consider making kitchen wreaths using fresh bay leaves, rosemary, thyme, sage and other woody herbs. These will slowly dry and you can use the herbs as you need them. You can also make colourful, aromatic kitchen wreaths from cinnamon sticks, cloves and dried orange slices (but if your kitchen is humid or damp, varnish the orange slices first – and don't eat them!).

Get Crafty

Traditional crafts have always been integral to the ICA. For many early ICA members, their craft skills were a means of income as well as a source of pleasure, whether sold through The Country Shop in Dublin's St Stephen's Green or through local Country Markets. Some say you can't teach an old dog new tricks, but we like to think that life-long learning makes young pups of us all. When the ICA was established in 1910, its aim was to improve the standard of life in rural Ireland through education and co-operative effort. Today our adult education centre, An Grianán in Termonfeckin, Co Louth remains a mecca for crafts lovers from all over the country, who come to undertake courses in everything from lacework, embroidery and crocheting to calligraphy, beaded jewellery making and felting. Here are a few simple ideas to get you started.

Crafty Kit

SELLOTAPE & GLUE: If you're using a roll of sellotape without a tape holder, a good trick is to pop a small coin under the loose end so that you can find the end easily the next time. Pre-used tubes of glue can be tricky to re-open, as the lid often sticks to the bottle. To avoid this, rub some Vaseline in the grooves before closing the tube. Or fit a piece of candle as a stopper to close the bottle. Glue does not stick to candle wax so you should no longer have any problems when you come to reuse it.

SCISSORS & BRUSHES: Scissors can be re-sharpened by cutting through a piece of coarse sandpaper several times. (This also works wonders with machine needles: simply sew a few stitches through sandpaper with an unthreaded needle.) Dried out, hardened brushes can be rescued by immersing them in hot vinegar for about an hour.

PINS & NEEDLES: Keep a small magnet in your sewing box; if you drop the pins on the floor while using you will be able to pick them up easily. Sometimes an ill-fitting thimble will keep slipping off smaller digits. To stop it falling off, simply suck your finger before fitting it on: the suction will hold the thimble in place. If you find your double thread keeps tangling when sewing, simply knot the ends separately instead of together.

Knitting & Needlework

Knitting has made a big comeback and is no longer seen as the preserve of elderly ladies biding time by the fire. But of course our elders always did have some useful tips up their sleeves to pass on to the next generation of novice knitters. While it can be a very relaxing and even sociable pastime, knitting does demand a certain concentration and focus. Organisation is the key to stress-free knitting. Instead of worrying about forgetting the required increases or decreases in your garment, simply pop a press-stud in at the end of each shaping row to mark it and remind you. Always wind the wool into balls with the label in the centre so that it is easy to check should you need to match a dye number. When knitting with more than one colour ball of wool, place the balls of wool in a plastic net vegetable bag and pull each colour through a different hole to prevent tangles. Alternatively you could use a regular plastic bag with small holes punched through.

Knit a Gift

This neck warmer makes a versatile present for Christmas, a birthday or any special occasion. It can be knitted quickly and is very comfortable to wear. Any chunky wool is suitable and one 100g ball will be more than sufficient. You can knit with 6mm, 8mm or 10mm needles.

Loretta's Neck Warmer

LORETTA SHERRY, MONAGHAN

1. Cast on 25 sts on 8mm needles; 21 sts on 10mm; or 29 sts on 6mm needles.

2. Row 1: Knit 1 Purl 2 (Knit 1 Purl 3) to last two sts, Knit 2.

3. Row 2: Knit 1 Purl 1 (Knit 3 Purl 1) to last three sts, Knit 3.

4. Repeat these two rows until work measures 23–25 inches.

5. Cast off 16 sts (12 sts, 20 sts), work in pattern remaining 9 sts (this will make the little loop to attach the button or brooch to). Work two rows of pattern. Decrease one st at beginning of each row until one stitch left – remember to continue work in pattern. Cast off. Sew up cast off seam to side seam. Add button, brooch or corsage as wished. (See below for a home-made rose brooch pattern.)

Crochet a Gift

This crochet project can be created with just a few scraps of DK (Double Knitting) wool, a 4mm crochet hook and a simple brooch back. You could create your own brooch back with a small circle of felt and a safety pin. This pattern will make a rose of about 6cm (2.5in) diameter, but see below for details on making alternative sizes. (Note that we have used British English crochet terminology as opposed to American English.)

Louie's Rose Brooch

LOUIE CLEMENT, WATERFORD

Stitches used:
Sl St – Slip Stitch
Ch – Chain
Dc – Double Crochet
Tc – Treble Crochet

1. With a 4mm crochet hook, make a slip knot leaving 10–12" tail, chain 41.

2. Row 1: Tc in 4th chain from hook. 2 Ch, 2 Tc in same space. *Ch 1, skip 2 chains. In next chain, 2 Tc, 2 Ch, 2 Tc. Repeat from * to end. Ch1, turn.

3. Row 2: Sl St into first Ch 2 space. 3 Ch, 6 Tc in same space. *Dc in Ch 1 space, 7 Tc in next Ch 2 space. Repeat from * to end. Fasten off.

4. Thread the tail of yarn onto a needle. Roll the crocheted piece that you made in a spiral shape so that the petals come together to resemble a rose. Sew into place. To finish, sew the brooch back to the back of the rose.

To make smaller roses and rosebuds, start with the following chain count:
Small rosebud – chain 12
Medium rosebud – chain 15
Small rose – chain 21
Medium rose – chain 34

Get Cooking

Everybody loves a sweet treat, but it's all the sweeter a gift if it was made especially for somebody. Even simple gifts like home-made fudge or biscuits can be given an extra special touch if packaged cleverly inside glass Kilner jars, wrapped with pretty tissue paper and tied with coloured ribbon. It doesn't have to be complicated to be impressive: something very easy like slabs of chocolate reset with fruit and nut toppings is a lovely way to tell someone you're thinking of them (see p147).

Home-made preserves are a great way to use up a bounty of home-grown fruit or vegetables, which tend to inundate the kitchen gardener in late summer and autumn. This makes them particularly good ideas for Christmas gifts for friends and extended family. Simply make up a batch with the fresh produce, label and store in carefully sterilised jars in a cool place. When Christmas comes around all you'll have to do is tie a ribbon on and away you go.

Back in the Day...

"When I was a small child most farmyards included an orchard. My mother had lots of innovative ways of using apples including apple cakes, apple tart, apple chutney, baked apples, apple snow and spiced apples to name but a few. The king of them all though was apple jelly and I have fond memories of coming home from school and the smell of the apples cooking on the range waiting out the door to greet me.

I would watch fascinated as my mother removed the warmed jam pots from the oven, poured the steaming golden liquid into them and then sealed them carefully with cellophane covers. I usually got the job of putting on the labels and then the pots were carefully put aside until they cooled. The next day they were placed in a dry cupboard to be used as required.

Today I continue to make the apple jelly, with the apples still coming from the remnants of our old orchard and following my mother's recipe in the same traditional way."

Patricia Cavanagh, Monaghan

Apple Jelly

Patricia Cavanagh, Monaghan

This makes a delightful present to give to family and friends and will last very well if you have sterilised your jars carefully. You can add a little whiskey to give it a bit of festive cheer, but the flavours are wonderful without it too. Try serving with roast pork or cheese, or spread on hot buttered toast.

makes about 5kg
(10 lb) jelly

INGREDIENTS
- 5kg (10lb) cooking apples
- 2 litres (4 pints) water, approximately
- 1 small handful cloves
- 2 cinnamon sticks
- 1.5kg (3lb) sugar, approximately
- 100ml (3.5fl oz) whiskey (optional)

what you'll need
- 8–10 jam jars
- 1 large preserving pan
- piece of muslin or jelly bag

ICA Tip
The strained liquid freezes very well and you can make the jelly direct from the frozen liquid using the above method. Allow to defrost fully and heat through before adding the sugar and returning to boiling point.

1. Wash the apples and remove any discoloured pieces. Chop roughly (no need to peel) and place in a large preserving pan. Top up with just enough water to cover the apples and add the cloves and cinnamon sticks.

2. Bring to the boil, reduce the heat and simmer for about two hours, stirring periodically to prevent the mixture from sticking and burning. You may want to add more water if the mixture looks too thick. The end result should be a nice runny consistency and should have reduced in volume by about one third. Meanwhile, pop a saucer in the freezer to chill.

3. To sterilise your jam jars, wash well in hot soapy water, rinse thoroughly and place still slightly wet in a cool oven for 30 minutes or in a microwave on full heat for 60 seconds. Alternatively, boil top-down in a large pot of boiling water for five minutes.

4. Strain the liquid through a piece of muslin or a jelly bag. (Do not force mixture through a sieve or you will have a cloudy jelly.) Measure the clear liquid before returning to the preserving pan, bringing the liquid back to boiling point and adding a pound of sugar for every pint of liquid.

5. Taking care that the liquid does not boil over, keep to a rolling boil until setting point is reached. The jelly sets very quickly as there's a lot of natural pectin in apples. To test for setting point, place a spoonful of liquid on a saucer pre-chilled in the freezer. When the jelly cools a little, a skin will form on the surface; this should wrinkle when pushed with your finger.

6. Remove any scum from the top of the pan with a slotted spoon. Stir in a little whiskey, if using. Pour the jelly into clean, warmed jars. (Remember: Always add hot jam to hot jars, never hot jam to cold jars or cold jam to hot jars.) Cover each jar with greaseproof paper tied with twine or secured with rubber bands. Label each jar, including the month of production as well as the name of its contents.

Fruit & Nut Bark

Elizabeth Murphy, Laois

These can look very pretty wrapped in transparent cellophane paper and tied with coloured ribbon, and make sweet little token gifts or stocking fillers at Christmas time. This recipe makes the equivalent of four bars of chocolate, but can easily be halved or doubled as needed.

INGREDIENTS

- 400g (14oz) dark or milk chocolate
- 6 handfuls dried cherries
- 4 handfuls mixed nuts, whole or roughly chopped
- 2 handfuls crystallised ginger

It's the Little Things…
"Clean the cooker hob before you start making jam, marmalade or jelly and wipe off any splashes as you go to avoid every little grease splash or dirty mark being baked on by the time you finish."

1. Bring a pot of water to a rolling simmer and place a heatproof bowl over the pot to create a bain marie. Chop the chocolate into chunks and place in the bowl to melt gently.

2. Meanwhile, line a baking sheet with greaseproof paper and combine the fruit and nuts in a mixing bowl. Stir half the fruit mix into the chocolate, pour onto the lined baking sheet and spread out evenly with a spatula.

3. Sprinkle over the remaining mixture evenly and transfer to the fridge to chill for about 10 minutes or until set. Break into pieces – any size will do, and it's nice to keep it a little irregular. Store in an airtight tin in the fridge or in a cool place until ready to wrap up as gifts. They will keep for about three weeks, if they last that long!

Chapter 7
Minding Yourself

TIME OUT · NATURAL BEAUTY · WEAR IT WELL

Time Out

When you are juggling the demands of modern living it can be very easy to put everyone else first and forget to look after yourself, but of course someone has to mind the minder too. That means prioritising your various needs and factoring them into your busy week. Look after yourself and your family will be looked after too.

Spend some time alone every day. Allowing yourself even 20 or 30 minutes quiet time every day will make you better able to give your love and attention to others around you. Set aside an afternoon every few weeks for 'me time', and use it to do whatever you feel like – whether that be to go to an art exhibition or movie, or treat yourself to a day of luxurious pampering. You don't need a lot of money to spoil yourself: there are plenty of DIY treatments using everyday items which can be found around most households. It's about taking the time for yourself as much as anything.

Friend in Need

It's so important to maintain friendships: our friends help us solve the worries of the world. Seek out a couple of good friends in life and hold on to them. True friendship is like health and the value of it is seldom known until it's lost. But the beauty of lifelong friendships is that those bonds are hard to shake. Don't let a little dispute injure a great friendship, and don't let the gaps between meeting up slip too far.

Take the time to keep in touch with friends, whether they are near or far. While social media, Skype and the internet make keeping in touch with overseas friends so much easier, there is still something special about receiving a handwritten letter or card. Set aside an afternoon in early December to write and send your Christmas cards, and update your diary every year with special friends' birthdays. Arranging a regular night out with a close group of friends is a good idea, and it doesn't matter whether it's for a book club or a poker night – any excuse will do!

Remember that having fun is important. Laughter stimulates the brain to produce hormones that fight disease and pain. Regular laughter is like an inoculation against disease. Hormones generated by laughter reduce tension and are good defences against the creeping onslaught of guilt and depression.

 My mother always told me: 'Self first, self last and anything left, self again'. You are the most important person in your family to be minded. If you are okay, your family will be okay.
Breege Lenihan, Monaghan

Bathtime & Bedtime

When we're going all day long it can be hard to stop at night. Part of the solution is to start slowing down before you get to bed, and a long lazy bath can be a great way to change pace.

A cup of Epsom salts added to a bath works like magic to soothe away aches and pains. To make your own scented bath salts, mix 250ml of Epsom salts with 250ml of sea salt, scent with 10–20 drops of essential oil and up to 10 drops of food colouring (red can give a pretty pink effect). Mix well and transfer to a glass bottle with a wide neck and tight-fitting lid. Lavender

oil is excellent for encouraging a good night's sleep.

If you don't have any essential oils to hand, you can also scent a bath with kitchen ingredients. Fill a net bag with fresh lemon or orange skins and let the water run through them as you fill the bath. The oils in the citrus will be good for your skin and the fragrance will give the bath water a delicious scent.

For a really good night's sleep, make up little sachets of lavender, hops or chamomile flowers – or equal quantities of all three. Place the sachet in your pillowcase where the heat of your head will help release the soothing essential oils.

Natural Beauty

Some of us love the pampering effect of expensive potions and lotions, but there are many very affordable alternatives to be found in your kitchen cupboards. If bathing in milk and honey was good enough for Cleopatra, it's good enough for us!

Skincare

It was not uncommon at one time to see farmer's wives pat their face with fresh buttermilk immediately after churning to help combat wrinkles. Few of us churn our own buttermilk today, so an egg white face mask is a more accessible alternative. Egg white is made up of water (which will evaporate from your skin) and albumin proteins. These proteins dry into a hardened mask; as it is removed it takes the loose dead cells with it, making the skin look smoother and healthier.

There was a time here in Ireland when olive oil could only be bought in the chemist. That may sound strange today, but you might be surprised by the effects gleaned from a bottle of olive oil, which can be used as a general body moisturiser, on your face in place of expensive anti-ageing serums or as a rich hair conditioner. All those antioxidants, anti-inflammatory properties and vitamins (particularly the skin-friendly vitamin E) make it a great base for all sorts of skincare treatments. Try blending with some ripe avocado for a nourishing face mask, with Demerara sugar and essential oils for an invigorating exfoliant or with oatmeal for a more gentle scrub. Lavender oil has anti-bacterial properties which make it great for problem skin (you can mix with water for a facial toner). Rose oil is great for mature or ageing skin or as a cleanser when mixed with water.

Mind the Pennies...
"Before applying expensive face moisturiser I always moisturise my hands thoroughly with cheap cream like Nivea or Cien (available in Lidl) to prevent my fingers absorbing the precious face cream." Emily McCarthy, Dublin

Caring Cucumber

Cucumbers are full of most of the essential vitamins and minerals, including vitamins C and B1, B2, B3, B5 and B6, folic acid, calcium, iron, magnesium, potassium and zinc. All that goodness makes for a great pick-me-up and a more sustainable fix for the mid-afternoon slump than caffeine. And together with the sugar and electrolytes they also contain, they are a healthy remedy for dehydration and related headaches. A few slices eaten before going to bed will help sore heads after a night out!

If you're stressed out and don't have time or money for a massage, facial or visit to the spa, there's a quick and easy treatment you can do at home. Cut up an entire cucumber and place it in a pot of boiling water: the boiling water will unlock the cucumber's chemicals and nutrients and release them into the steam, creating a soothing, relaxing aroma which is thought to reduce stress. Fresh cucumber slices placed on the eyelids also help to soothe tired eyes.

Hands

Washing, rinsing and wringing; chopping, dicing and slicing; digging, scrubbing and wiping: our hands do so much for us around the house that they really deserve a little attention and kindness in return.

To save your manicure before attacking a dirty job in the kitchen or the garden, scrape your nails over a cake of soap. Bleach can leave your hands slimy as well as smelly, so pour a little vinegar or lemon juice over your hands and rinse well. The acid of the vinegar and lemon neutralise the alkaline of the bleach, and help to rebalance the pH of your skin.

Of course, investing in a decent pair of rubber gloves is also an excellent idea for protecting hands from the harsh effects of cleaning chores. Shaking a few drops of olive oil into each glove before donning allows you to enjoy a simple but effective beauty treatment while working. Your hands will be lovely and soft when you finish all your hard work.

It can be harder to protect against the smells and stains that come with the preparation of certain foods. Garlic, onions and fish odours particularly love to linger. Rubbing salt into wet fingertips helps draw out the smell of onions, as does rubbing with mustard or sugar and washing in warm water. Garlic odours can be neutralised by rubbing your hands on anything stainless steel – a sink or bowl, a large spoon or even the flat of a cook's knife. To remove fruit stains from your hands, rub them with a little vinegar and wipe with a cloth.

Don't throw out lemon and lime wedges that have been squeezed of their juice. Keep them beside the sink and use to rub on your hands after handling fish. Regular cleansing with lemon will also bleach age spots and nicotine and false tan stains as well as strengthening nails and removing dead cuticles.

During the cold winter months our hands can become very dry. For very rough hands, try scrubbing with equal parts butter and caster sugar. Equal quantities of lemon juice and glycerine is a soothing treatment for chapped hands while cobbler's wax will help cure cracks in your fingers. To revitalise the hands, pour a teaspoon of salt onto the palms, moisten with a tablespoon of any cooking oil and massage thoroughly. This will leave hands feeling smooth and warm. Rinse off and follow up with a nice hand cream.

Feet

Never mind that a good foot scrub makes wearing open sandals a more attractive prospect whenever our sunshine decides to show up: treating your feet well is also a great way to feel a little pampered. Tired feet can be rejuvenated in a basin of hot water with two teaspoons of bicarbonate of soda, while soaking feet in warm water with vinegar helps to whiten toenails and to combat smelly feet. (Remember that cotton socks aid odour control more effectively than woollen ones.) For a simple exfoliating scrub, mix up a handful of oatmeal with some almond or olive oil and apply to skin in circular motions to get rid of dead skin. Rinse off and for extra pampering, coat the hard skin on your feet with Vicks and don a pair of socks going to bed.

To remove callused skin from feet, first bathe them in warm water and pat dry. Then halve one or more sultanas and place the cut side on corns. Position in place with a plaster. Continue this treatment until the corn can be easily removed. An inflamed bunion can be particularly painful. Crushing a few aspirin tablets into a basin of water and soaking your feet for 10 to 15 minutes can bring some very welcome relief (but if any skin irritation results, discontinue the treatment).

Haircare

Treat your hair to an old-fashioned conditioning treatment for a rich shine. Beat an egg until light and frothy, apply all over the hair and massage through. Cover with a shower cap and leave for at least half an hour, then rinse out the egg. Shampoo and style the hair as you normally would.

Another traditional treatment for hair that lacks vitality may sound less appealing but is very effective. Melt the marrow from a bone of beef in a double saucepan. In a separate saucepan, heat 150ml (¼ pint) of warm rum together with a generous sprig of rosemary to infuse. Blend the rum with the bone marrow and apply to the scalp, massaging lightly. Wrap your head in a towel and leave for an hour or two before shampooing thoroughly.

Nettle tea makes a lovely hair rinse that promotes shine and growth and leaves hair well-cleansed. It can also soften the texture of grey hair and relieve itchy scalps. To make your own shampoo, simply immerse the nettles in water, bring to the boil and leave overnight to cool. You can add some chamomile to the infusion for a blonde-friendly brew, ginger for redheads and sage for brunettes. The next day, strain off the herbs and return the remaining liquid to a gentle heat. Grate in about a tablespoon of Castile soap to melt. Allow to cool fully before transferring the mixture to a clean bottle, where it will keep for a month or two.

After shampooing, rinse the hair with a solution of water and lemon juice (for blondes) or apple cider vinegar (for brunettes and redheads) to remove any soapy film and give hair a beautiful shine. If you suffer from dandruff, try rubbing a mixture of olive oil and eau de cologne into the hair and rinsing thoroughly.

If you don't have time to wash your hair but it needs a freshen up, talcum powder makes a handy quick fix. Sprinkle in a tablespoon of the powder, dust gently through your hair to absorb some surplus oil, and brush out after three minutes.

Brushes, Curlers & Cuts

Dirty brushes can make your hair dull, so be sure to clean them regularly. A teaspoon of borax and a tablespoon of washing soda in warm water will keep hairbrushes clean and fresh, or you can soak them in a vinegar solution.

If your hair is very soft and fly-away, try dipping your comb in milk. Alternatively beer makes an excellent setting lotion. Apply before blow-drying or putting rollers in your hair. If you want to set it overnight, remove the plastic clips from sponge hair rollers and replace with lengths of pipe cleaner so that you can wear rollers in bed with comfort.

Many believe that the moon cycle influences growth cycles in our bodies as well as in our gardens. To encourage your hair to grow thicker, it is said to cut it when the moon is waxing and D-shaped. To make your hair grow longer, opt for a cut when the moon is waning and C-shaped.

Wear It Well

It goes without saying that if you don't look your age you certainly don't want your clothes to. Nothing ages clothes faster than not being properly cared for. Invest in a clothes brush and in one of those nifty gadgets for de-bobbling sweaters. Always read the care labels and hand-wash or dry clean where appropriate. Clean, well-pressed clothes should always be hung up or neatly folded, never crammed into over-stuffed wardrobes. Always air clothes after a night on the town before putting them back in the cupboard. Store winter coats and jackets in separate clothing bags to prevent dust collecting on collars and to keep them fresh. Dry clean items such as coats at the end of the winter before you put them away.

Make sure you buy the right clothes in the first place. Never buy something for the sake of a 'bargain' and only buy clothes that fit perfectly and make you look and feel good. It's false economy if you never wear it. Be sure to try clothes on before buying and forget the size label. Every shop sizes their clothes slightly differently, so you may find you need to take your usual size and one smaller or bigger into the changing room to get the right one.

Caring for... Your Precious Jewels

Store a piece of camphor in the box with your chunky jewellery to prevent tarnishing and to keep the stones bright.

Rub gold with soft white bread to bring up its shine. For a deeper clean, soak overnight in a glass of cola. Rinse and dry.

Buff up silver jewellery by rubbing with half a lemon and rinsing well.

Soak diamond rings and earrings in gin for a thorough clean that will make them shine and sparkle.

Wrap costume jewellery in tissue paper with a piece of white chalk to prevent tarnishing.

Maintain Your Footwear

1. Clean spots of dirt from glossy leather with a damp sponge. Scuff marks can be removed with a shoe polish of the correct colour.

2. Baby wipes are a quick and handy way to put the shine back on your leather shoes. For a deeper polish, clean patent leather shoes with Vaseline and buff off with a clean, soft cloth or an old pair of tights.

3. Polish leathers regularly and use a waterproof and stain-protector spray on suede and fine leather.

4. Stains on suede shoes can be eased off gently with a nail file. Fresh white bread is also useful for cleaning suede or felt slippers. Simply rub it all over the slippers: as the crumbs fall away, the dirt will too. Repeat until they are perfectly clean and shake off the surplus crumbs.

5. If new leather shoes are hurting your heels, help break them in by rubbing dampened soap on the inside. Or try storing shoes stuffed with peeled potatoes to stretch the leather naturally.

6. Where possible, store your shoes and boots stuffed with paper or shoe trees to help them keep their shape.

7. Don't let heels or soles wear down too far, but rather always re-heel and re-sole shoes as soon as they're worn.

8. You can significantly extend the life of leather shoes by applying silicone fluid, available in your local chemist.

9. To deal with smelly shoes, sprinkle bicarbonate of soda into them. For the stinkiest of trainers, fill with a sockful of cat litter and leave outdoors overnight to neutralise the powerful odours.

10. Slippery shoelaces can be rubbed with candlewax or simply wiped with a wet cloth to help secure the knot.

Chapter 8
Caring

FEED THEM WELL · TRADITIONAL CURES
CARING FOR GUESTS · CARING FOR PETS

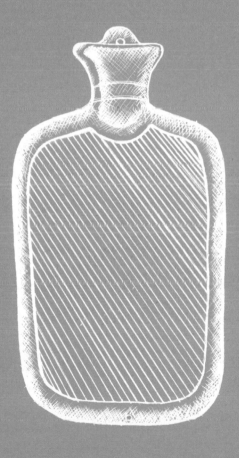

Feed Them Well

It's no news to most parents that paying attention to what your family eats can greatly improve our general health, but we can still learn a lot from our own mammies' approach to nutrition.

Back in the Day...

"I smile to think of what they used
To help us kids survive,
But I am going on 69 and very much alive.
My sorest throats were eased,
And I still hold no bit of rancour
To think of sucking sugar lumps
With a drop or two of camphor –
And camphor mixed with goose grease
For a winter chest congestion.
Baking soda cleaned my teeth
and helped my indigestion.
Because of mother's tender heart
I hearby sing a Gloria:
She never gave me castor oil,
Just syrupy castoria.
Salt for all mosquito bites,
Cobwebs on the scratches,
The sick room fumigated with
Our sulphur kitchen matches.
Somehow there's quite a bunch of us
That never had a shot –
But here we are still kicking
And enjoying it a lot."
Author Unknown,
via Phil Kiernan, Westmeath

Herbs for Health: an A-Z

ALOE VERA: Good for burns, scalds, eczema and as a laxative. Mix the gel into a steam inhalation for bronchial relief.

BASIL: Good for stomach pain and nausea. Mix one teaspoon of fresh or dried basil in a cupful of warm water, drink, and repeat once or twice a day.

Ideal with pasta, tomatoes, fish dishes, chicken stuffing, Mediterranean foods, stews, and egg and cheese dishes.

BAY LEAVES: Good for soothing systems from the effects of over-indulgence. Make tea from bay leaves.

Use in soups, casseroles, marinades, sauces and stuffing.

CHAMOMILE: Good for digestion and aids sleep. Tea made from the flowers assists digestion and chamomile flowers added to a hot bath before bed helps to ensure a relaxed sleep.

CHIVES: Good for digestion and iron deficiency.

Chop and sprinkle on salads and other foods. Good in omelettes, scrambled eggs and chopped finely over new potatoes.

DILL: Good for soothing an upset stomach and easing hiccups. Make an infusion from the fresh or dried leaves.

Flavours meat loaves, meatballs, soups,

sauces, cold vegetables and fish and egg dishes.

FENNEL: Good for bathing sore eyes, relieving headaches, blocked sinuses and rheumatic pain. Make tea from fennel seed infused in hot water.

Adds flavour to sauces and salads, most meats and fish. The seeds can be sprinkled on plain scones before cooking to give them an aniseed flavour.

GARLIC: Good for reducing blood pressure and cholesterol, fighting infection and aiding digestion. Use two or three cloves each day in cooking.

Ideal for Italian dishes, stews, chicken, fish, salads, egg and vegetable dishes, garlic bread and potatoes.

LAVENDER: Good for agitation. Drink a tea made from the flowers and leaves for a gentle sedative.

MEADOWSWEET: Good for flu, fever and arthritis. Infuse a tea from the dried herb and drink one cup daily.

Add to jams and stewed fruit to lend a slight almond flavour.

MINT: Good for indigestion and vomiting. Drink one cup of mint tea daily.

Mint sauce is a traditional accompaniment for lamb, but use also for cheese, chutneys and salads.

NETTLE: Good for dandruff and hair loss, and full of iron in springtime. Make a tea from the boiled roots and rub into the scalp daily.

Can be used as a cooked vegetable (soak prior to cooking to draw out the sting).

OREGANO: Good for morning and travel sickness. Sip a tea made from oregano leaves.

Add to salads, sauces, pasta dishes, pizza, meat, chicken and egg dishes.

PARSLEY: Good for digestion, rheumatism, kidney and bladder trouble and the sympathetic nervous system in general. Rich in iron, calcium and vitamin C. Eat raw as a great breath freshener or steep chopped leaves and stems in hot water and drink daily.

Use for fish dishes, egg and cheese dishes, fried, roasted and barbecued meat.

Back in the Day…

"In times past, nettles were traditionally taken on Ash Wednesday and Spy Wednesday as a tonic. When the fresh nettle shoots came up, our mothers would harvest them and wash them well before boiling and straining. The liquid was then given to us children to drink. It tasted dreadful but mother insisted that we take it to 'clear our blood'. Another way of getting the good of the nettles was to chop them up finely and mix and cook with cabbage. Some families chopped and cooked the nettles and passed it off as spinach."

Ballinode Guild Members, Monaghan

Traditional Cures: an A-Z

Modern medicine has achieved so much, but there is still a lot of sense in some of the old tried and tested cures – and there's no harm in helping your body help itself.

Some of the old cures might be less palatable than others, particularly to those more used to a modern diet. There may not be many today who would happily stomach a mug of buttermilk to cure an upset stomach caused by excesses the night before. The traditional cure for a toothache – to soak a piece of cotton wool in whiskey and bite down on the affected tooth – may prove a little more attractive to some!

ARTHRITIS: Ireland's favourite food contains anti-inflammatory properties. To help with arthritic pain, boil potatoes, mash them, place in muslin and apply to the affected area until cool.

BLOOD PRESSURE: The juice of boiled beetroot will help to lower your blood pressure. Garlic or evening primrose oil are also good, and chewing dandelion leaves helps reduce fluid retention.

BURNS: Dab a few drops of pure aloe vera gel on the burn. If you do it quickly enough, you will have no blister and the pain will disappear. (Aloe is also great for mouth ulcers – just dab it on the sore spot and forget about it.)

CYSTITIS: One or two glasses of cranberry juice a day can prevent and treat painful cystitis, and help flush out the system.

EYE INFECTION: For sore eyes and minor infections, soak a piece of cotton wool in cool chamomile tea and apply directly to the eye, leaving on for a few minutes. Alternatively just or use a chamomile tea bag. To cure a sty in the eye, bathe with cold tea.

FOOD POISONING: The cooking water from white cabbage is high in sulphur and helps to fight the bacteria which might be causing minor diarrhoea and nausea. You could eat the cabbage itself too but make sure it is well-cooked so that it is easy to digest.

HAY FEVER: Chew a small piece of honeycomb for 20 minutes up to five or six times a day. Continue treatment for at least three weeks or until the symptoms pass. Alternatively drink a teaspoon of cider vinegar in a glass of water every morning.

INDIGESTION: Bring half a pint of milk to the boil with a pinch each of nutmeg and pepper, sweeten with sugar or honey and drink it warm.

INSECT BITES: Onions and lemons have a cooling and disinfecting effect and will reduce the swelling caused by insect bites. Simply place a slice of either onto the bite or sting and position in place with a plaster.

MOSQUITOES: To deter mosquitoes from biting you, focus on eating foods rich in vitamin B1 including cereals, porridge, brown rice, nuts, dairy and red meat. Garlic is helpful too.

RHEUMATISM: Steep four large cloves of garlic in a pint of brandy for ten days. Take half and half in a glass of water first thing each morning for rheumatic pains.

SINUS TREATMENT: Each morning sniff a mild saline solution of one teaspoon of salt to 250ml (½ pint) of water through one nostril at a time.

SKIN RASHES: Add a cup of bran to your bath to alleviate severe itching. Rosewater is also good for treating rashes. Mix 250ml (½ pint) of rosewater with 125ml (¼ pint) of lemon juice and dab the solution onto the rash several times a day. To soothe heat spots, nettle rash and chicken pox, apply a paste of bicarbonate of soda and water.

SORE THROAT: Fill a nylon stocking with warm salt and place on throat.

STIFF JOINTS: Goose grease or fat is recommended to rub into stiff joints. (Goose grease is also great for polishing your shoes or boots!)

STINGS: Use vinegar on a wasp sting and bicarbonate of soda on a bee sting.

SUNBURN: Cool sunburn by soaking in a bath of lukewarm water topped up with a cupful of vinegar. Spray regularly with ice-cold vinegar to deter blistering and peeling.

TOOTHACHE: Soak a piece of cotton wool in whiskey and bite down on the affected tooth.

UPSET STOMACH: Bring a glass of water to the boil and allow it to cool, and then stir in a teaspoon each of bicarbonate of soda and sugar or glucose. A teaspoon of bicarbonate of soda is good for neutralising acid heartburn.

WARTS: For warts on hands and fingers, apply the white liquid from the stem of the dandelion flower. Alternatively mix equal parts glycerine and cider vinegar into a lotion and apply daily. Sudocreme rubbed on warts will shrink them.

Extreme Cold

We don't often have very cold weather in Ireland so we are not well-versed on how to protect ourselves, but there are some simple things we can do.

In very cold weather, whether coming from a warm car or house, on the first step outside your door, stand still until the soles of your shoes acclimatise to the cold. This helps to prevent your warm shoes melting the surface ice or snow, which carries a risk of slipping.

If you are stepping out of a heated car, swing your feet out and place on the cold road as you sit in the car and count to twenty to allow your soles to get cold.

If you are carrying appropriate shoes to change into before you leave the car, keep them in the main car and not in the boot. Likewise keep a pair of shoes outside the door or in an unheated porch.

Dress for the weather. Layers are the solution, with one layer of wool over one cotton and a wind breaker on the outside.

Mittens are better than gloves for preserving heat. Wear a wool hat that is light on the head but keeps you warm, and consider doubling up on hats when it is very cold.

Drink warm water and eat small amounts often in order to preserve body heat.

Cure a Cold

1. We have forgotten many of the old remedies for winter colds and flu, even though we have nothing much to put in their place. Despite all the advances of modern medicine, there is still little which can be done about the unpleasant side effects of these viruses, and so we soldier on, taking the odd aspirin or hot medicated drink, and feeling sorry for ourselves.

2. A glass of hot punch gives at least temporary relief because the inhalation of steam makes breathing easier. Cloves help to relieve pain, and ginger can be added to the drink to assist in cleansing the system. The other traditional flavouring is nutmeg, which is a mild 'pick-me-up'. A tablespoon of blackcurrant jam can be dissolved in a mug of boiling water, stirred well and strained for a tasty hot drink.

3. A tea made from fresh thyme was once commonly used for colds, laryngitis and whooping cough. To make it, steep a heaped teaspoon of the picked leaves in a half cup of hot water for five minutes. Strain and take one or two cups a day, sipping a mouthful at a time.

4. Sage tea makes a good gargle for sore throats, laryngitis and tonsillitis, but it is safer not to swallow it as it can be poisonous in large doses. To make the tea, steep one teaspoon of leaves in half a cup of hot water for thirty minutes.

5. Make your own cough syrup by gently cooking six roughly diced white onions in a double boiler with a half cup of honey for two hours. Strain and take at regular intervals, preferably warm. For a tastier alternative, heat together two tablespoons each of brown sugar, lemon juice, brandy and honey.

Caring for Guests

We are all so busy these days. Mothers and grannies have fulltime jobs, parents are taking children to sports, music and other cultural pastimes as well as running the house, and so our free time is often limited. But it is no less important to have get-togethers and to keep in touch with friends and family. Entertaining for family and friends can be satisfying and enjoyable – a pleasure for both the guests and the hostess – but it does help to give it some forethought.

Choose meals that can be prepared ahead or at the last minute with a minimum of effort. A good rule of thumb is to aim for one hot course, one cold and one that can be prepared well in advance. It is better to serve simple food that is well-presented than to attempt a complicated spread that needs a great deal of attention. Never forget that your guests actually come to see you and will want to relax with you. If you are in the kitchen frantically basting and chopping this won't happen.

Houseguests

Having houseguests to stay can be a real treat if you're well-organised, and can work both ways: you get to have a mini-holiday too as the pace in the house takes on a different swing. But it's no holiday for you if you leave everything to the last minute. And it's no holiday for them if they go without a comfortable night's sleep or a nutritious meal.

People's likes and dislikes are worth considering. Most adults will cope discretely with slight dislikes but check diets before houseguests arrive so that you can cater accordingly. Roast spuds and veg while everyone else is tucking into rare roast beef does not make for the best vegetarian option. Some friends will bring their own 'specials' if they have a particular health problem, fad or dietary preference such as vegans and vegetarians or coeliacs.

When you are having visitors for the weekend it is even more important that meals are prepared in advance (at least partially) and need the minimum of last minute action, such as pushing something into the oven. Choose some simple desserts such as cheese or fruit or home-made ice-cream that can be served straight from the freezer. Keep main courses filling and serve with easy-to-prepare salads or vegetables.

If you are going to be out all day, put a casserole or lasagne in the oven on an automatic timer, or leave stews and casseroles to work away in a slow-cooker. Alternatively, leave some fish or meat to marinate (lamb kebab meat in a spicy sauce or chicken breasts in a tandoori paste maybe) so that it can be quickly grilled off when you get home, and served with salad or French bread.

Meals for Visiting Children

Many children today have very sophisticated tastes in food and more often than not will eat what the adults are having, which makes things considerably easier. However, not all children share adults' tastes in food so if you have a mixed party it might be best to serve the children separately.

Fill them up with something reliable that most children enjoy (checking with the parents is a good idea): home-made beef burgers, or chicken and wedges served with salad are reasonably healthy possibilities.

For a mixed group where it is not practical to have separate menus, it is better that there is a compromise. The children's needs and tastes really have to be met first or no-one will enjoy the party.

Giving the adults child-friendly foods rather than the other way round can be the simplest solution.

If you serve the children first, they can always come back for bits of the grown-up spread afterwards. This way the parents can relax knowing the children are fed and won't be demanding attention. Depending on the weather you can serve them picnic foods such as slices of wholemeal pizza or quiche and fruit flavoured yoghurts. Small rolls of ham, cheese and other salad foods can be supplemented with baked potatoes or wholemeal bread or rolls. If the weather is warm enough, make up a personalised 'tuck box' for each child and send them out into the garden to eat; they will love the adventure – and their parents will love the break.

Make the Perfect Cuppa

1. We Irish take our tea very seriously, and though we are primarily a nation of tea-drinkers, many of us take our coffee seriously too. There is an art to the making of a perfect cuppa, and as with most things, cleanliness and hygiene are important factors.

2. Teapots should be kept stain-free, as the deposits will have an effect on the flavour of the fresh tea. Fill with warm water, pop in a denture cleaner tablet and leave overnight. Alternatively, boil rhubarb in the teapot to clean it thoroughly. To keep a teapot fresh when not in use, wash and dry thoroughly and place a few sugar cubes inside.

3. To descale a kettle from lime deposits, fill it with water, add a tablespoon of vinegar or lemon juice, bring it to the boil and rinse. Allow to cool and rub the inside with a cloth to remove scale. A stone placed in the bottom of the kettle will collect the lime and can be easily changed when needed.

4. When making fresh coffee, avoid pouring freshly boiled water over or you may scald the coffee grounds, resulting in a bitter taste. Leave the kettle for a minute after it has boiled before pouring. Tea, on the other hand, should be made with just-boiled water and the teapot itself should be scalded by pre-heating for a few minutes. Loose leaf tea yields a more nuanced flavour than teabags. If using teabags, never squeeze them as this encourages bitter tannins.

5. Tea is best drunk out of fine bone china and many insist that the cold milk be poured into the cup first so that it is less affected by the heat of the tea. For coffee, however, milk should be heated before serving. Rinsing the pan with cold water before doing so will prevent the milk sticking to the sides of the pan.

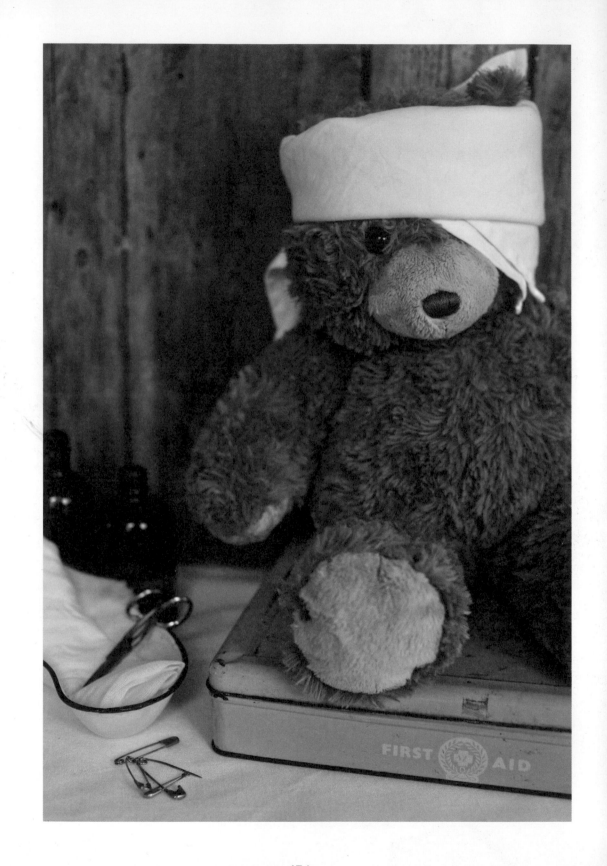

Caring for Pets

Fleas are no fun for anyone, be they owners or pets. A dose of vinegar added to your dog's or cat's drinking water will kill off fleas. You can also wash their coat in a weak solution of vinegar and water, sprayed or rubbed on, and use it neat to wipe out a dog's ears to stop him scratching.

General pet odours can be persistent and hard to shift. Cat litter trays should regularly be cleaned out thoroughly and disinfected with a thumbnail width of vinegar in the base of the tray. Soak for half an hour and rinse well with cold water. Of course the smells are even worse if they don't use the litter tray. To deal with the odours of a pet's 'accident', clean the area thoroughly with warm, soapy water and then cover liberally with bicarbonate of soda. Leave it overnight, hoover up the soda and re-wash the area with white distilled vinegar. Rinse and leave to dry.

When cleaning out aquariums and fish bowls, you can recycle the water for your houseplants (see p132). Shift any deposits and grime left on the glass by soaking with vinegar and rinsing very well before re-filling.

Prepare a Guest's Bedroom

1. It's important to anticipate that your guests may have different needs to you. Some of us love a toasty bedroom, while others are used to a fresher environment for sleeping. Ensure that a window can be opened easily in the middle of the night (from the inside only, of course – you don't want them awake with worry) and radiators switched on or off if needs be. Equally, provide extra blankets in the bedroom should they be needed in the night.

2. A jug of water beside the bed and fresh clean glasses is a considerate touch, especially if you'll be having a couple of drinks over dinner. The water will keep fresher for longer if you add a sprig of fresh mint. Tissues, a nightlight, matches and a fresh set of earplugs are also thoughtful (especially if you live near a busy road).

3. A good reading lamp is important, especially for elderly guests whose eyesight might not be what it once was. You might consider hand-picking a couple of good books from your shelves if you know what kind of reading material they are likely to enjoy. Maybe a book of short stories, some poetry and even one of your favourite cookbooks too. Even if they don't read them, the thought will be appreciated.

4. Spray guests' sheets and pillows lightly with lavender water (made up with essential oils) to help them sleep soundly. When you're making up the bed remember that not everyone likes to sleep in tightly tucked sheets. Don't tuck in too far so that they can be easily loosened if needs be.

5. If your guests are early risers and you are not, be sure that the heating immersion is set early enough for them to have a hot shower when they wake, and provide them with your fluffiest towels. Ensure too that they know their way around the kitchen, or maybe leave a pot of porridge soaking overnight which they can just cook through in a matter of minutes.

Chapter 9

Things We Wish We'd
Known Long Ago

" Don't try and be perfect – the perfect cook, the perfect housekeeper, the perfect mam – as you'll simply wear yourself out and make your home a less happy place. Remember that everyone is just as unsure about their parenting skills and style as you are. Relax and do your best. Don't necessarily listen to your mother-in-law. And don't get a puppy when you have a small child in the house – you won't have the time or energy to train it properly and it will just become one more onerous chore. Resist the cuteness! "

" The golden rule is 'do unto others as you would have them do to you'. Basically this means that you should treat other people with the same concern, kindness and respect as you would like them to show towards you. Give your friends, family, neighbours and even strangers your time, help and friendship when they are in need – who knows when you might need the same from them. "

" Remember: a bird never flew on one wing. "

" Strangers are just friends waiting to happen. "

" If you find a friend who is just and true, don't ever part the old for the new. A friend in need is a friend indeed. "

" Tell me your company and I'll tell you what you are. "

" Friends are better than gold but a constant guest is never welcome. "

" Good fences make good neighbours. "

" You can choose your friends but you can't choose your relations. "

" If you're tempted to speak ill of someone, consider taking a coal off the fire instead of piling on another one. But if you do have something to say, stand up and speak out instead of muttering. Stick to the truth and you will not go far wrong. "

" A closed mouth gathers no feet. "

" Don't ever slam a door, you may want to go back. "

" What forgets is the axe, but the tree that has been axed never forgets. "

" It's nice to be important but more important to be nice. "

" You can't live a positive life with a negative mind. Counting your blessings, rather than constantly going over your complaints, makes for greater personal happiness and success. "

" Don't hold on to grudges. There will always be someone who has hurt or angered you, but by holding on to that injury you only hurt yourself – not the person who hurt you. "

" Nobody can make you feel bad unless you let them. Believe in yourself; nobody else will unless you do. "

" Love many, trust few, always paddle your own canoe. "

" Be happy with what you have while working for what you want, and remember that nothing comes into a closed hand. "

" If you want to mix you have to stir yourself. "

" Never venture, never win. There is no gain without pain. "

" Our greatest glory is not in never falling but in rising every time we fall. He who does not hope to win has already lost. "

" The one thing worse than a quitter is a person afraid to begin. You never know what you can do until you try. "

" The harder you work the luckier you get. "

" Cut your own wood and it will warm you twice. "

" Hope for the best but always plan for the worst. "

" There is a story about four people named Everybody, Somebody, Anybody and Nobody. There was an important job to be done and everybody was sure somebody would do it. Anybody could have done it, but nobody actually did it. Somebody got angry about that because, after all, it was everybody's job. Everybody thought anybody could do it but nobody realised that anybody wouldn't do it. It ended up, as it often does, that everybody blamed somebody when nobody did what anybody could have done. "

" Give everything your best and you'll always come away satisfied. "

" Wilful waste makes woeful want. Live simply that others might simply live. "

" Remember that everyone is the same underneath the skin. "

" Be the living expression of God's kindness; kindness in your face, kindness in your eyes, kindness in your smile, kindness in your warm greeting. "

" All this will last short. Time never gets tired of running." "

" Remember to take note of things your parents or grandparents pass on to you. It's too late when they are gone and you will have no recipe for the lovely mayonnaise or Christmas pudding they used to make. Record the family tree while you have someone who remembers and who can verify the various people and their relationship with your family. Listen to your elders' stories and jot them down: it's only after several years that you will become really interested and you will be so glad to have captured some of it. "

" The older the fiddle the sweeter the tune. "

Contributors

The ICA would like to thank all the Guilds and individual members who sent in their treasured tips, advice and words of wisdom passed down through the years and gleaned from life experience.

Ada Vance, Cavan

Aine Reynolds, Leitrim

Alice Carleton, Cork

Aloma McKay, Clare

Ann Bolger, Kilkenny

Ann Dwyer, Laois

Ann Gilmartin, Mayo

Ann McCann, Meath

Anna Connolly, Donegal

Anna Egan, Roscommon

Annascaul Guild Members, Kerry

Anne Cass, Laois

Anne McDonagh, Westmeath

Anne O'Connor, Wexford

Anne Payne, Laois

Astrid Moffett, Monaghan

Aughadown Guild Members, Cork

Ballinode Guild Members, Monaghan

Ballyroan Guild Members, Laois

Barbara Meer, Mayo

Beltra Guild Members, Sligo

Bernie Ducker, Mayo

Bernie Judge, Mayo

Bernie Keating, Waterford

Bernie McAndrew, Mayo

Beth Holmes, Wicklow

Betty Gorman, Laois

Breda McDonald, Kilkenny

Bree Guild Members, Wexford

Breeda Hennessy, Tipperary

Breege Haugh, Mayo

Breege Lenihan, Monaghan

Brenda Daly, Carlow

Brid Fitzpatrick, Kilkenny

Bridie McGinty, Mayo

Brigid Keane, Waterford

Cappamore Guild Members, Limerick

Carmel Yore, Meath

Caroline Power, Meath

Castletown Guild Members, Laois

Catherine Leavey, Westmeath

Catherine O'Sullivan, Cork

Celia Cahill, Laois

Connie McEvoy, Louth

Deirdre Connery, Wexford

Deirdre McCormack, Monaghan

Delores Devereux, Wexford

Drogheda Guild Members, Louth

Eileen O'Callaghan, Waterford

Eileen Treacy, Galway

Eilis Bailey, Galway

Eilish McDonnell, Westmeath

Eithne Lee, Wexford

Elizabeth Kelly, Meath

Elizabeth Murphy, Laois

Ellen Hanna, Leitrim

Emily McCarthy, Dublin

Ena Howell, Cork

Francis Thorn, Wexford

Gertrude Kenna, Kilkenny

Gretta Kelly, Meath

Heather Evans, Tipperary

Horace Plunkett Guild Members, Meath

Horseleap Streamstown Guild Members, Westmeath

Jackie Slattery, Clare

Jane Johnston, Longford

Jennifer Sloane, Dublin

Joan Hayes, Limerick

Joy Burns, Longford

June Lawless, Dublin

Kathleen Gorman, Laois

Kathleen Kelly, Longford

Kathleen Leinster, Cavan

Kathleen Murray, Dublin

Kay Devine, Mayo

Kay Murray, Clare

Lily Champ, Laois

Lismullen Guild Members, Meath

Liz Wall, Wicklow, ICA National President

Loretta Sherry, Monaghan

Louie Clement, Waterford

Louisa Cuthbert, Louth

Maghera Guild Members, Cavan

Mai Hendy, Laois

Mairead McAuliffe, Wexford

Margaret Bowkett, Wexford

Margaret Grennan, Sligo

Margaret Murphy, Waterford

Margaret O'Hara, Mayo

Marion Lawless, Laois

Mary Bergin, Kilkenny

Mary Butler, Kilkenny

Mary Dunbar, Sligo

Mary Feehan (RIP), Louth

Mary Fitzgerald, Wexford

Mary Fitzpatrick, Kilkenny

Mary Gallagher, Mayo

Mary Harkin, Sligo

Mary Harley, Donegal

Mary McWey, Laois

Mary O'Griofa, Waterford

Mary O'Malley, Mayo

Mary O'Neill, Wicklow

Mary O'Reilly, Mayo

Mary P Maher, Kilkenny

Mary Timmons, Carlow

Maureen Davey, Sligo

Maureen Mullarkey, Mayo

Nancy Phelan, Kilkenny

Norah McDermott, Kildare

Nuala Beale, Laois

Patricia Cavanagh, Monaghan

Patricia Kehoe, Wexford

Patricia Larkin, Mayo

Pauline O'Callaghan, Cork

Peg Prendeville, Limerick

Peggy Curran, Monaghan

Peggy Lyons, Monaghan

Phil Kiernan, Westmeath

Phillis Roe, Meath

Rockchapel Guild Members, Cork

Rockcorry Guild Members, Monaghan

Rooskey Guild Members, Roscommon

Rose Fitzsimons, Cavan

Sally Dunleavy, Mayo

Sarah Buckley, Wexford

Sarah McDermott, Monaghan

Sharon Kelly, Galway

Sheila Baynes, Mayo

Sixmilebridge Guild Members, Clare

Stephanie Igoe, Longford

Susan Ryan, Kildare

Theresa Storey, Limerick

Two Mile House Guild Members, Kildare

Una Flynn, Westmeath

Winnie McCarron, Monaghan

Acknowledgements

It is wonderful to see The ICA Book of Home and Family come to fruition. What began as a small idea in my head has been realised for all to enjoy and to pass down through the generations.

I am extremely proud of our members and to have been involved with this project from Day One. Collectively, the ICA women are a mine of information. Now the world can witness just how much wisdom they have to offer, and that wisdom can be put to good use in many more homes around the island of Ireland and beyond.

I would like to thank each and every contributor for their invaluable material without which this book could not have come into being. I also wish to thank the following people for all of their help:

Joanne Dunne for her professional handling of all submissions and her ever-cheerful liaising with the editor.

Rebecca Ryan for her helpful proof-reading.

Edward Hayden for his generosity, attention to detail and good judgement in helping to test the recipes.

Ada Vance for her extensive contribution to the kitchen-related material.

Kathleen Gorman for her guidance in relation to the gardening material.

Joanne Murphy for her atmospheric photography and Blondie and Carly Horan for styling the photographs and capturing the essence of this book.

Aoife Carrigy for her hard work and dedication and for the extensive hours that she has put into this book along with all her patience and support.

Finally, to all the team at Gill & Macmillan for their endless support in creating another book that the ICA can be extremely proud of – thank you.

Liz Wall, National President of the ICA

Index

A

acidic stains 30, 35
adages 4, 5, 8, 9, 20, 150, 180–81
aioli 74
air fresheners 3, 47
Alka Seltzer 134
all-purpose cleaner 19
allergies 19
almond icing 102
aloe vera 164, 166
aluminium 51
ammonia 30, 37
angora 34
Annascaul Guild 29
annual planner 14
ants 128–9
aphids 119
apples 56, 57, 145
    Apple Jelly 146–7
    Kerry Apple Cake 91
    pancake filling 72
    storage 128
aprons 4
aquariums 175
Aran sweaters 34
arthritis 165, 166
ashes 24, 25, 26, 50, 127
aspirin 36, 155
asthma 19, 46
avocados 56, 152
azaleas 127

B

Baby Bio 118
baby oil 42, 52, 64
baby wipes 35, 160
bain marie 50
Báirín Breac (Barn Brack) 95
Baked Ham 81
Ballinode Guild 165
Ballyroan Guild 44
bananas 56, 58, 72
    as fertiliser 117, 127
basil 164
bath salts 152
bathrooms 29, 42–4
bathtubs 30, 42–3
bay leaves 47, 164

bed linen 37
bedrooms 45–6, 176
beech leaves, preserving 132
beef, Haymaker's Beef 87
beer 24, 25, 156
beetroot 166
bicarbonate of soda
    as carpet cleaner 27
    as cleaner 19, 22, 24, 30
    as deodoriser 3, 30, 33
    and egg substitute 74
    as fridge deodoriser 48
bins 47
bird feeders 131
birds 129
birthday cakes 110, 111
birthday parties 108
black spot 119
blackberries 72
blankets 36
bleach 33, 35, 43, 134
blood pressure 165, 166
blood stains 30, 35
blueberries 72
bone marrow 155
book shelves 29
borax 27, 28, 30, 43, 128
boric acid 28, 43
Bowkett, Margaret 110
Boxty 104
brack, Báirín Breac 95
brass 22, 24
bread
    leftovers 58, 96
    soda bread recipe 77
    storing 57
bread bins 46, 57
breakfast, Full Irish 106
breastfeeding 9
breath freshener 165
Breda's Family White Soda
    Bread 77
broccoli 47, 56
bronze 24
brown sugar, softening 58
brushes 142
    for dusting 20
    hair brushes 156

    paint brushes 64
    toothbrushes 43, 24
Buckley, Sarah 76
budgets 9
bulbs 118, 131, 132
burns 28, 164, 166
Butler, Mary 5, 20
butter, making 78
butterflies 128
buttermilk 35, 78
    Buttermilk Pancakes 71

C

cabbage 47
cakes
    Christmas Cake 101
    Kerry Apple Cake 91
    No-Bake Chocolate Biscuit
        Cake 111
    No-Bake Ice-Cream Birthday
        Cake 110
    storing 57
camphor 25, 159, 164
candles 3, 62, 160
candlesticks 3, 24
cane furniture 24
carnations 134
carpets 27–8
carrots 56, 118
Casey, Julie 32
casserole dishes 52
cast iron pots 30, 51
Castletown Guild 81
cat litter 3, 47, 160
cauliflower 47
Cavanagh, Patricia 100, 145
ceilings, washing 29, 64
chalk 62, 64, 129, 159
chamomile 127, 152, 156, 164, 166
Champ, Lily 88
charcoal 48
cheese 57, 58
chewing gum 35
chickens 120, 122
children 8, 9, 108
    birthday cakes 110–11
    meals for 171
    toilet training 42

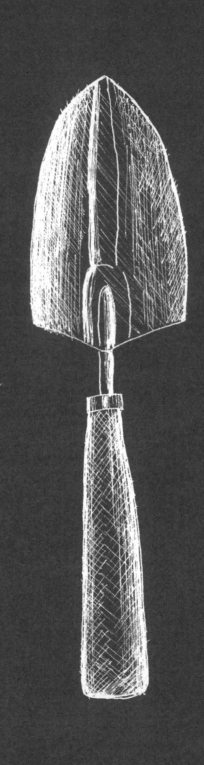